A wise old friend
once said that days spent fishing
aren't deducted from life.

SMOKY LIGHT FROM FIRES OF 1988, NEZ PERCÉ CREEK, YELLOWSTONE NATIONAL PARK, WYOMING BY LARRY ULRICH.

STREAMSIDE REFLECTIONS

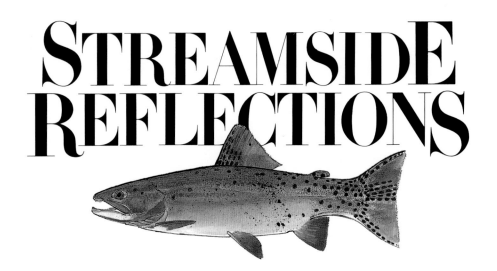

SCHWABACHER LANDING ON THE SNAKE RIVER, GRAND TETON NATIONAL PARK, WYOMING BY PAT O'HARA.

STREAMSIDE REFLECTIONS

FLY-FISHING FOR TROUT AND SALMON

WRITTEN BY STEVEN J. MEYERS
PRODUCED BY McQUISTON & PARTNERS

THUNDER BAY PRESS, SAN DIEGO

I t is well known that a better river always lies just a little farther over the horizon. But if we can't reach that next river, no matter, for it is equally well known that in the river you are fishing, a better pool is just around the next bend, and a better fish will always come on your next cast.

Above: rainbow by Tom Montgomery; right: Tuolumne River, Yosemite National Park, California by Larry Ulrich.

FISHING FOR STEELHEAD ON THE UMPQUA RIVER, OREGON BY TERRY RING.

To I. Edward Meyers

Like a river or a stream, a book springs from a central source. In this case, it was Thunder Bay Press, San Diego, where Charles Tillinghast and Craig Schafer had a vision of this book that happily meshed with ours. And so did many others. Steven Meyers's sensitive essays reveal a dedication to the sport that is best described as a healthy fanaticism. Jack Unruh's superb illustrations clearly document his enthusiasm for the project. We are indebted to John Dawson for his hospitality and for an introduction to Silver Creek. John Van Derhoof provided some much-needed guidance in addition to his fly-tying skills. Bob Marriott of Bob Marriott's Fly Fishing Store gave generously from a rich fund of knowledge. We are grateful to Jim and Padraic Stroud for sharing their late father's fly rods and reels. The editing skills of Frankie Wright and Robin Witkin made an invaluable contribution to the text. Dr. Robert Behnke was extremely helpful in providing information on trout nomenclature. Datus C. Proper lent us his thoughts on differences between fly designs and patterns. A special word of gratitude goes to the talented men and women whose photographic images grace the pages of this book: R. Valentine Atkinson, Jim Brandenburg, Willard Clay, Jeff Gnass, Tom Montgomery, Pat O'Hara, John Oldenkamp, Terry Ring, Cynthia Sabransky, David Stoecklein, Donna Ulrich, Larry Ulrich, Jim Vincent, and Kitty Pearson-Vincent.

And finally to Hollis Holland, Louie Neiheisel, and the late Tully Stroud—thanks for being good fishing buddies and the best of friends.

—McQuiston & Partners

Library of Congress Cataloging-in-Publication Data:
Meyers, Steven J.
    Streamside reflections: fly-fishing for trout & salmon
    p. cm. Bibliography: p.
    ISBN 0-934429-18-9
    1. Fly fishing. 2. Trout fishing. 3. Salmon fishing.
I. McQuiston & Partners. II. Title.
SH456.M48 1990 799. 1'755—dc20 89-80490 CIP
10 9 8 7 6 5 4 3 2 1

Photo Credits
Cover: Snake River, Grand Teton National Park, Wyoming by Larry Ulrich
Frontispiece: by R. Valentine Atkinson/Frontiers

Printed in Japan by Dai Nippon Printing Co., Ltd.

Published by Thunder Bay Press
5880 Oberlin Drive
San Diego, CA 92121

UNNAMED LAKE, WIND RIVER RANGE, WYOMING BY TOM MONTGOMERY; OPPOSITE: DOLLY VARDEN BY JIM VINCENT.

TABLE OF CONTENTS

STEELHEAD FISHING, SMITH RIVER, JEDEDIAH SMITH REDWOODS STATE PARK, CALIFORNIA BY LARRY ULRICH.

INTRODUCTION

Angling history is a long history, full of colorful characters and tales, technical innovation, and introspection. Documented in a rich body of literature, this history fills the shelves of our libraries with volumes of both fiction and nonfiction. Visual artists, too, have sought inspiration in the themes of angling. Images of fly-casters on mist-shrouded rivers, of shimmering trout leaping from a stream to snare insects on the wing, are familiar to all of us. Idyllic scenes of pastoral beauty often include a trout stream, an angler, or both. Art is the embodiment of the ideals and aspirations of a culture. It is no accident that angling is so much a part of our aesthetic traditions.

When we began fishing many thousands of years ago, we fished for food. Not until more recent times did we begin to fish for fun. The majority of fish taken are still taken for food, and most of the methods devised for catching fish reflect this simple fact. Netting and trolling, for example, yield great quantities of fish and are used by commercial fishermen to make a living, and to feed others. This is not sport. It is hard work. And its lore, too, is rich.

But this is not angling. Angling is the catching of fish with a fishing rod, a line, and a hook. Because angling is by no means the most efficient way to harvest fish, something other than the mere catching of fish must be involved. This other thing is our love of beauty.

The notion of beauty can be quite a can of worms. The beauty of which I speak, however, is not the controversial concept of the aesthetician, but the knowledge in the gut that makes us gasp before a sunset or stand quietly in a dappled wood. This knowledge belongs to all of us; for many of us it is affirmed in the act of angling.

Our choices regarding quarry and method reflect this knowledge. Angling is indelibly associated with a family of fish and a style of fishing: trout and salmon and the fly rod. No fish, I maintain, are as beautiful, and no fishing implements as elegant, and no technique as graceful.

A wise uncle once said to me, "Don't bother with excuses. Your friends don't need them, and no one else will believe them." I suspect the pragmatists, realists, and modernists will regard all of this flowery speech on angling as so much fluff, another useless piece of maudlin sentimentality. So be it. Those of us who angle for trout and salmon, those of us who choose to fish the fly, need make no excuses—neither for our behavior, nor for our language. And I'll let you in on a little secret: Though an awful lot of serious talk goes on about the aesthetics and ethics of angling, most of these thoughts sit below the surface, for the most part, while we fish. We fish because it's so much damn fun. Sometimes, however, we just can't help wondering why.

This book is a celebration of the joy and beauty of angling, but I hope that it will be something else as well. The rich history of fly-fishing, the wonderful joy so many of us find on the trout stream, the abundant life that makes trout populations and salmon runs possible can all, very easily, come to an abrupt halt. Trout and salmon habitat face degradation by careless agriculture; hasty timber harvests; industrial development; hydroelectric projects; air, soil, and water pollution; and countless other threats. In places where habitat has been protected, entire runs of anadromous fish are endangered by overzealous, saltwater harvesting. Healthy trout streams often have their best breeders removed by thoughtless fishermen. Issues relating to the complexities of genetic preservation and the spread of non-native species need examination, and resolution. To revel in the pleasure of this sport is not enough. Unless we become involved in the protection of fish and habitat, a time will come when angling is nothing more than history.

One of my favorite thoughts involves the image of my child walking the banks of one of my favorite streams with a child of his own. I see him handing one of my favorite fly rods to his own son or daughter as I watch. I see them casting in the clear water, under a deep blue Colorado sky. Large, healthy, cutthroat trout rise to mayflies that hatch in great numbers from the water. Trout sip flies from the surface, occasionally taking an artificial fly, bending an old rod, making an old reel and an old man's heart sing. It is unimaginably sad to think that my generation's greed and shortsightedness might make this dream an impossibility.

15

LYMAN LAKE, GLACIER PEAK WILDERNESS AREA, WASHINGTON BY PAT O'HARA.

16

Yellow Creek, California by R. Valentine Atkinson/Frontiers.

Few moments in life are as full of hope and expectation as the instant we first gaze upon a stream we will spend the day fishing.

Silver Creek, Idaho by Kitty Pearson-Vincent.

The first cast carries our fly, and our hope, into the world of the trout. The next move belongs to the fish.

18

Most anglers have a few secret spots, places they know big fish hide, places they believe few others have fished. Many times these secret places are beaver ponds. Beaver ponds are inconsistent from one to the next, and it's difficult to know what you will find in one until you have fished it. Once good trout are located in a pond, it becomes a treasure. Some anglers greedily hoard such places, while others swear a few friends to secrecy and share the bounty.

Above: cutthroat trout, Wind River Range, Wyoming by Tom Montgomery; right: Elk Creek, Colorado by Larry Ulrich.

20

BLACK RIVER, WHITE MOUNTAINS, APACHE NATIONAL FOREST, ARIZONA BY LARRY ULRICH.

THE HOME STREAM

England has some streams that call to mind images of wealthy gentlemen with little to do but to sit on stone benches alongside rich chalk streams, waiting, watching the water for signs of a rise. The Test. The Itchen. Home waters to men born into wealth and to some rather heated debates—the dry fly versus the wet fly, and conflict about the ethics of each. In our daydreams Frederick Halford and G. E. M. Skues, theoreticians, anglers, ghosts of an age long since passed, still stalk the fat brown trout of British chalk streams.

To fish in the shadow of kings. To fish for the king of all game fish. Fishing for Atlantic salmon in Europe meant more than having money; often it meant having the position of birth, social status, or contacts that would allow one to purchase fishing rights along one of the established salmon rivers in Norway or Scotland. The Tweed and Spey bring forth images of fine woolens and a stylish kind of roll cast done with a long two-handed salmon rod. The Alta, the Vossa, the Laerdal and Aroy are Norwegian salmon rivers with pedigrees and histories that run parallel to the great families of Europe. They have hosted some of the most colorful (and wealthy) fishermen who have lived. Charles Ritz, of the famed Ritz Hotel in Paris, was a salmon fisherman who is better known in the outdoor fraternity for his angling exploits in Norway than for anything he ever did in the hotel business.

North America has spawned its own angling lore. European settlers brought with them their love of trout, of salmon, and fished the rivers where they lived. As the dubious benefits of civilization became more and more evident on this continent, we too developed a class of people who, if not always wealthy, were able to angle for more than meat; we too developed a history of famous rivers and streams, of fishermen who left behind a good deal more than the bones and viscera of fish they had eaten; we too had great debates about fishing ethics and methods; we too became a part of the history of angling.

The fabled rivers of the Catskills were the first home of the truly American fly—the Catskill School dry flies of Theodore Gordon. These same rivers were the home of Edward Ringwood Hewitt, our first great fisheries theorist. The Beaverkill and the Neversink became rivers easily the equal of the Test and Itchen, if not in length of history, certainly in their importance as places of American identity and affection.

The Brodheads in Pennsylvania's Pocono Mountains gave us Jim Leisenring, a man of legendary stature, both physically (he was a big man) and historically, who turned the fishing and tying of the wet fly into an art. Samuel Phillipe, the father of the modern split-cane rod, also fished there.

An American equivalent to the chalk streams of England is found in Pennsylvania: the limestone streams of the Cumberland Valley. Primary among these great streams is the famous Letort where Vincent Marinaro, until recently, fished for difficult brown trout. This is the birthplace of the American terrestrial imitation—the fly that imitates not the aquatic insects (mayflies, sedges, or the caddis flies and other imitations we inherited from the English), but the land-based insects that sometimes end up in our trout waters accidentally: jassids, beetles, grasshoppers, crickets, and ants. These flies, now used worldwide, are a mainstay on waters everywhere and are particularly popular (in big, bushy, high-floating form) on the brawling waters of the American West.

Ah, the American West. Few places stir the mind so. Up near the Yellowstone country, in Montana, Idaho, and Wyoming, are countless trout rivers. They vary in character as much as the tortuous and upthrust mountains and plateaus through which they flow. The Yellowstone and Firehole rivers run headlong downstream through a geology as surprising as any in the world. Early anglers in this amazing country loved to tell the tale of catching a trout in a cold mountain stream, flipping the line and fish into a geothermal pool nearby, and eating a steaming poached fish, all without having to move a step.

The Henry's Fork of the Snake River, the Madison, the Gallatin—all of these names stir the blood of the American angler, generating happy daydreams about that trip we have made, or hope to make someday. These rivers have their heroes too: Dan Bailey, who left the tame East to fish and make a name for himself on the waters of the West, and Charles Brooks, who argues that anglers trained in more dainty ways had better learn to fish big flies deep if they hope to catch any of the really sizable trout these burly waters hold.

The American Northwest is the home of other famous rivers and anglers, home to strong and sleek sea-run rainbow trout, the steelhead, and to anadromous salmon born in the gravel beds of rivers with outlets to the ocean. It is the land of the Umpqua, the Rogue, and the Deschutes rivers, water where Fred Burnham, a giant figure in the history of steelhead fishing, taught Zane Grey how to cast the fly for these powerful fish.

History and famous rivers form a substantial part of the lore and attraction of fly-fishing, but for most of us such places remain distant dreams or only rarely visited waters. Most of us spend the better part of our angling careers in the familiar currents of home.

Most of us have a home stream, the place, I suspect, where we are most happy.

Home streams are received in various ways.

Some of us (not very many any more) live where generations of kinfolk lived before us, and because of the depth of existing roots, are able to inherit the tales, the game, the fish, the woods, the streams—the place. The home stream is a given, a birthright. For most of us though, the home stream is something we find long after childhood, after years of wandering and seeking, after we have cast many thousands of flies, held and released countless quivering trout, after we have walked, sniffed, touched, and been touched in return by many a wood, many a stream. Eventually we find a place where we feel strangely comfortable, and when we find it, we also find the birthright we were initially denied—a birthright we had been dimly aware of, even in its absence. A home stream, however we receive it, is a home.

I guess I'm luckier than some. I live in a part of the world where trout streams, most of them quite good (a few even famous) are plentiful. I can easily fish, and often do, rivers with a substantial pedigree. The Gunnison and Arkansas of Colorado and a piece of the San Juan in northern New Mexico are in this category. I can hike to the headwaters of the Rio Grande or drive to the more accessible water a few miles downstream from the Continental Divide. The Dolores River very near to home is rapidly gaining a national reputation after its conversion to

23

superb fishing water in some of its lower stretches (stretches of water that once were home to warm water species) after the McPhee Dam and its cold water discharge appeared a few years ago. The Animas, another good trout river, flows a few hundred yards from my front door. Other trout water flows nearby. The Pine, the Piedra, the Florida. Yet none of these is my home stream, and although I spend a good deal of time on these waters, that special place where the water seems as familiar as my living room and as comfortable as my worn moccasins, is a smaller, more intimate stream than any of these. It is Lime Creek, about thirty miles north of home, in the southern San Juan Mountains.

I can still remember, as if it were yesterday, the first time I fished there. Much of my time that summer had been spent hiking to and then fishing the lakes of the Weminuche Wilderness. (Fishing seems to hit with periodic obsessions, and that summer my obsession was high altitude lakes. Streams and rivers had been temporarily forgotten. The obsession was decent enough and had all of the ingredients of neurotic behavior: everything else was forgotten; I lost sleep thinking about it; I worried about the work that wasn't getting done—but it was fun!) One day, after a lengthy binge of lake fishing, I ran into a good friend who wanted to go fishing but had little time to get away. He suggested a quick trip

to Lime Creek. I had hiked to it many times, but had never cast a line there (too close to home; not enough adventure). Thinking it wouldn't be much of a fishing trip, but expecting a good time with an old friend in spite of it, I decided to go.

When we got there, about an hour before sunset, tiny brook trout were rising in the broad, shallow, slow-water pools. They readily took small dry flies. It was easy, so easy in fact, that once, while we were talking, enjoying the night air and each other, our lines trailing in the water as we spoke, we lifted our rods and gathered in line, preparing to move on, only to find that each of us had a brookie thrashing about at the end of his leader. It was more than easy, it was friendly. Hollis and I separated to see if we might find some bigger fish in the faster water, in the deeper pools along the undercut banks. We did.

Fishing this water wasn't exactly difficult, but it wasn't a place where you could be careless either. The trout were there—rainbows, a few cutthroat—and they were beautiful, brightly colored, sharp-finned, wild trout. Spooky. Cautious.

For the next month in the orange and yellow low-angled light of autumn, I fished Lime Creek, learning more about the valley, the woods, and the trout. Many of those fish were caught several times. Soon, previously unknown pools became familiar places, inhabited by familiar fins, by bodies with familiar markings. Looking into the eyes of a trout repeatedly over the course of time is a very different thing from having your paths cross, and having the opportunity to gaze, just once.

Complex currents became friendly waters. Stones and boulders, which once hid beneath the surface turbulence and caused me to stumble as I waded along the streambed, became as familiar as the rugs on the wooden floors of my dwelling (on which I had also stumbled, until my house became a home). I came to know much, to feel comfortable, to

expect certain things to be there when I arrived.

And after years of fishing there, I found that fishing elsewhere, while also quite wonderful, was quite different. I would fish the gentle, easy flow of Lime Creek immediately after a trip to the brawling currents of the Black Canyon of the Gunnison. I could be satisfied with the quiet familiarity of Lime Creek after exciting journeys to more fabled waters. No matter where you've been, it's always nice to come home.

25

26

Lost Creek, Lassen Volcanic National Park, California by R. Valentine Atkinson/Frontiers.

Savvy anglers approach the banks of spring creeks with caution. Sometimes large trout will feed in open water; more often, however, they hold against the bank enjoying the double benefits of food in the currents and cover from predators. A stealthy approach and a careful cast close-in often yield excellent results.

Gibbon River brown, Yellowstone National Park, Wyoming by Kitty Pearson-Vincent.

The reward, a handsome trout weighing heavily in the net, is not won through carelessness. Like all rewards worthy of the name, they come because they are earned.

28

Lake outlet, Wind River Range, Wyoming by Tom Montgomery.

It's amazing what an angler will do if he thinks it will help him find a fish.

Lake outlet, Wind River Range, Wyoming by Tom Montgomery.

Should a good fish be taken from a precarious perch the risk seems worthwhile, but the trip back to shore is infinitely more painful if all the leaping, hopping, and slipping have yielded nothing more than wet sneakers and a wounded ego.

Moments between casts, between trout, are some of the most glorious in angling. The warmth of the morning sun on the face after a dawn of frost and frigid air; the glint of dawn's russet light on streamside growth; the startled flight of duck or bounding retreat of deer; each is as welcome and carefully savored as the powerful tug of a strong fish at the end of the line.

Above and right: Bighorn River, Montana by Tom Montgomery.

32

Silver Creek, Idaho by Tom Montgomery.

A successful angler often differs from others who are less successful in one critical attribute: patience. But the patience of the angler is not a patience that suffers boredom. Angling patience is the patience that comes from paying attention to details during those slack moments the less attentive call empty.

Martis Creek, California by R. Valentine Atkinson/Frontiers.

Surprisingly large fish are often taken from the undercut banks of narrow, braided water.

34

SNAKE RIVER AT DEADMAN'S BAR AND THE GRAND TETON, GRAND TETON NATIONAL PARK, WYOMING BY LARRY ULRICH.

THOUGHTS SPAWNED BY A FAVORITE FLY ROD

The purpose of fishing tackle, at least as it appears on the surface, is to allow us to catch fish. But efficiency is not the only consideration. Herein lies the distinction between *fishing* and *angling*.

As a matter of primary definition, fishing is catching fish by any means; angling is catching fish by means of a hook. But I am drawn to a definition of angling given a bit farther down on the dictionary's list: "to use artful means to obtain an objective." Artful. Angling, then, is not simply the catching of fish, but choosing to catch them in a certain way.

Artfulness contains an inherent notion of beauty, which is difficult to define. Beauty really has little to do with any objective evaluation of appearance. Look at the way we see our

dogs as beautiful. Or take a look at our mates. No, beauty has little to do with appearance.

Consider my favorite fly rod. It has a name: Mergantroider. This particular craziness was not my fault. My son, who was five at the time, came up with the name, and I just didn't have the heart to tell him it was silly. Over time, however, I have come to regard it as strangely appropriate. Mergantroider is, well, a Mergantroider. Daniel, as usual, had been right.

Mergantroider was built one winter when I had a lot of things on my mind. I'd spent hours in the previous weeks filling my fly boxes, and I'd read every trout-fishing book I could borrow, or could justify buying. The streams and lakes were under ten feet of snow, and a trip to New Zealand was out of the question, so I decided to build a new rod.

I already had a pretty fair mess of rods. Fly rods run in line weights from one to twelve. The lighter rods (ones to sevens) are usually considered trout rods. Eights and nines will find use for steelhead, salmon, and perhaps the largest of trout (these are also considered good rods for bonefish); the rest, the heaviest rods, are meant for big game and casting large flies long distances to saltwater species, like tarpon. I had rods from four to nine weight, but my favorites were my fives and sixes, which makes sense, because the flies I usually toss and the fish I usually hook are best handled by these weights.

At the time my rods in the five- and six-weight category were limited to a wispy little eight-footer (for 4–5), a beefy eight-and-a-half-footer (for 6–7), both of graphite, a nine-foot fiberglass, which was as old as the hills and hadn't been fished since its original owner, Jim Bell, retired it a few years earlier. (I managed to inherit this rod from this very special man, and while I never fish it, I often take it out, hold it, and think about Jim fishing the streams of heaven.) I also had a crisp but delicate seven-and-a-half-footer made of split bamboo and originally designed for an HDH line, which was then, and still is, my favorite small creek rod. What I wanted was a long, light rod that would be more versatile than the 4–5 or the 6–7. What I really needed, or so I thought,

was a 5–6. What, in fact, I *did* need was a way to feel involved with trout and the trout stream, even though it was the dead of winter.

After many wonderful evenings of poring over catalogs and debating the pros and cons of various rod parts, I ordered an eight-and-a-half-foot graphite blank designed to balance a five- or six-weight line, a ceramic stripping guide, a rosewood reel seat, some corks, some thread, a new jar of rod varnish (my old one had a crust on its surface a half-inch thick), and a set of snake guides.

This new rod, I thought as I began construction, would be a thing of beauty. But for some reason (eagerness, I suppose), I made some pretty terrible mistakes on that rod. The varnish, for example, seemed to find dust in a room where I thought dust had been eliminated. The delicate tipping of the guide wraps, a light green used to contrast with the dark green of the main wraps, disappeared on the black rod blank when the varnish was applied— I had forgotten to use a color preservative.

The worst blow of all, however, came when I first tightened the reel seat. As I held the cork grip and twisted the up-locking seat, I heard a gentle pop, then watched as the cork began to rotate around the rod blank. I had forgotten to rough up the blank with sandpaper before gluing the rings, and the glue bond had broken. This meant cutting off the cork, removing the wraps and guides from the bottom half of the two-piece rod, and starting over. Sometime after the dust in the varnish and before the cutting off of the cork grip, it dawned on me that even though this new rod might someday prove serviceable, it was never going to be particularly beautiful. The name Mergantroider fit.

The rod took awhile to get used to. Its action was slower than my other graphite rods, and it was lighter and longer than my cane rod of the same line weight; but I soon came to like the gentler rhythm, slower line speed, and the more open loops it seemed to cast when I went through motions that were most natural for me. With this rod I could feel the line moving in a way I never had before. In a word, the rod fit.

I built Mergantroider to fish on medium-sized rivers and creeks. When spring finally arrived, that's what I did, and frequently. Later, I found myself taking the rod along on trips where in the past I would have used others. Instead of the heavy nine-footer I previously used for fishing from the canoe, I fished Mergantroider. Instead of the slightly heavier rod I had used for nymphing, Mergantroider became my rod of choice. I used this rod more and more, the others less and less. Now as I look back, I realize that I may fish the rest of my rods, collectively, as little as ten or twenty times a

year. In a good year I may fish Mergantroider nearly a hundred. I've replaced the guides and revarnished the wraps many times. The rod is scratched so badly in places that I often wonder when the terrible day will come that the blank will fracture under the load of a good fish or from too hard a push when straining for a long cast. Though it bears the gouges of many a tumble on the rocks, many a trek through dense undergrowth, the wear of too much use and too little rest, the many signs of a long, hard life; though the grip is worn and the varnish cloudy; Mergantroider is to me a thing of wondrous beauty.

37

38

Lincoln Creek, Aspen, Colorado by Willard Clay.

Trout are loved for what they are, I guess, but it's hard to separate them from the places where they are found. When people ask me why trout are so special, I always answer, ''Just look at where they live!'' Who can resist the feeling of being knee-deep in cold, rushing water? Who can resist a cool mountain breeze carrying a scent of moss and wet soil, or a streambed littered with the splintered fragments of surrounding peaks? Even if there were no trout, we'd be hard pressed to find a better place to spend a day, a week, or a life. But there are trout, and that makes it even better.

Photograph by Terry Ring.

The delicacy and beauty of the mayfly are obvious. The beauty of a stream may be readily apparent, but sometimes its delicacy is not. It takes little to disturb the tenuous balance that sustains aquatic life. The most sensitive indicator of environmental degradation is often the mayfly. Where mayfly hatches are prolific, other elements of the trout's world can often be assumed to be healthy as well. When mayfly populations dwindle, far more than mayflies are endangered.

40

Steelhead, Deschutes River, Oregon by Jim Vincent.

We've all heard serious talk about the reasons why we angle. Introspection seems to grow in trout water as comfortably as fish, but when you get right down to it, we fish because it's just so damn much fun.

Brown trout, Rangitikei River, North Island, New Zealand by Tom Montgomery.

Many moments in angling can be awkward—casting in the wind can put a fly in your ear, for example. Often the moment of netting or tailing a large fish is hurried, and that, too, becomes awkward. A big fish, no matter how you handle him, is a handful.

42

High altitude camps have many pleasures, and one of the greatest is fresh trout for dinner. Contemporary fishermen are well aware of the dictum "limit your kill, don't kill your limit," but there are times and places when it is appropriate to keep some of the catch. Where populations are healthy and regulations allow, nothing is better than freshly caught trout for dinner. Some of my favorite sunset memories are filled with the reflection of an evening sky in the clear water of an alpine lake, a jagged panorama of high mountains, and the piquant smell of trout, butter, onions, and peppers simmering together over an open fire or camp stove.

Above: catch from Rock Creek, Montana by Larry Ulrich; right: Big Martha Lake, California by Larry Ulrich.

44

Rangitikei River, North Island, New Zealand by Tom Montgomery.

Many of our most vivid memories have nothing to do with things seen. There's a trout swimming around in the bottom of the Gunnison River, for example, that haunts me still. He took a nymph in deep water, turned into the current, and ran without hesitation. My rod was deeply flexed, and my reel screamed, but he never slowed down. I never saw him, but I remember him better than hundreds I have seen. There have been others—steelhead who raced away with roaring rivers, browns who fled into tangles of weeds and roots. That these fish, these experiences, are so indelibly marked on the mind is further proof (as if any were needed) that angling is about a great deal more than just catching fish.

Green River, Utah by Tom Montgomery.

Brookies are Robert Traver's favorite fish. I can see why. Their colors are at once brilliant and subtle. They fight valiantly and with incredible persistence. No matter that they aren't actually trout, little brookies give life to many a small local creek. Big ones fill the rivers and lakes of remote northern lands. Someone once said of Traver, "When better fishing stories are written, Robert Traver will write them." I suspect he might have replied, "When better fish are made, they'll be brookies."

46

ANDROSCOGGIN RIVER, CAMBRIDGE BLACK MOUNTAIN, NEW HAMPSHIRE BY WILLARD CLAY.

JOURNEY TO THE EAST

Journeys to the East are associated in our minds with enlightenment, and I suppose that is proper. Many in my generation have found a new perspective, even wisdom, by traveling to Asia. I've never been to the lands of Buddha or Krishna, but a wise friend once told me not to worry, the trout are good teachers too. *My* journey to the East was made to the land of Pennsylvania, and there is no doubt in my mind that it was a significant journey.

Three of us made the trip, a simple American family driving across the continent to visit relatives and friends. But to me, the expedition was more than a vacation; it was a pilgrimage to holy water. Our path took us through the home of the infidel—once we left Colorado, we would not see trout water until

we arrived at our destination—and I suffered as a pilgrim should. We finally got there, to the promised land, and as we rolled down the highway, labored up the hills, and wound through the mountains, I began to feel pretty good. Pennsylvania was a little like home.

Days passed with friends and family. We canoed on the beautiful tree-shaded rivers of the East. But both Karen and my son Daniel knew I was chomping at the bit, waiting for my chance to try the trout streams near Carlisle. A day was set aside for trouting, and trouting alone, and at last, my visit to the holy water would take place.

This was my first visit to Pennsylvania to fish, and as any angler knows, there is no substitute for local information. I was staying in Harrisburg with my brother and his family, and I knew that Bob Clouser (of Clouser's Crawfish and Clouser's Hellgrammite fame) owned a fly shop nearby. I left early one morning to get a fishing license and some advice. When I found Bob, we had a nice conversation about the bass water on the Susquehanna, the wonderful fishing up on the West Branch of the Delaware, and trout and bass conservation. When it became clear to him that I was interested in some limestone fishing, we got serious about flies and choice of water. It was a little late in the season, and the Letort, he said, would be pretty weedy. Because this was my first trip, he suggested I try something not quite so difficult. He sold me a bunch of nicely tied little rusty midges (I also picked up some thorax-tied duns and some of his crawfish for my fly collection), then he sent me off with a hand-drawn map that would get me to the public water on the Yellow Breeches at Allenberry.

Now Bob was a nice guy and we had a great little chat, but he is also a fisherman, and he didn't know me from Adam. I knew he wasn't about to send me to his favorite spot, and the place he did send me was pretty nice, but, boy was it different from what I normally fished. For those of you who haven't been there, I'll try to describe the Yellow Breeches at Allenberry.

Trout streams, at least in my neck of the woods, are usually arrived at by driving down two-lane blacktop until your butt gets sore, then over rutted gravel until your kidneys ache, and finally (if it's a stream you can drive to) moving in a slow crawl through roadside brush and deep muddy ruts on a narrow dirt track until you can find a spot wide enough to park the car without blocking the road. When you get there, you get out and pee. You pull on your waders, scramble through willows and berry bushes, bite the thorns from your fingers and palms, free your rod tip from the undergrowth (a couple dozen times), and finally, exhausted, you find the river.

Allenberry is a little different. After driving through the elegant and beautiful Pennsylvania countryside, you come to a perfectly maintained, paved turnoff framed by two stone pillars. The turnoff guides you into a complex of stone buildings (theater, lodge, restaurant, gift shops), at the near edge of which is a parking lot with a sign. The sign reads: *Fishermen's Parking*. In the lot you see some very nice automobiles with license plates from all over the East.

As I crawled into my waders—all the while secretly wishing that the spot was more secluded so I could have jumped behind a tree to take a leak (because even though the road was not a kidney bruiser, I hated the idea of getting into waders without going to the bathroom; pulling on waders is a

48

known biological trigger for the voiding reflex, something from our distant, sea-going mammalian past I think)—I wondered what I had gotten myself into.

I figured that Allenberry, though different, must obey the same laws of physics as the world I knew in Colorado, so I walked downhill hoping it would take me to the stream. As I waddled across the perfectly manicured lawn (between the theater and the tennis courts), I passed a good number of friendly, soft-spoken people, all of whom said a kind hello. Some elderly couples strolled on the lawn, a few solitary individuals rested on stone benches overlooking what turned out to be the bank of the river, and in the distance I could still hear the gentle *puck, puck* of tennis balls striking the sweet spots of properly strung and swung tennis rackets.

At this point in its course the Yellow Breeches has been cleared of brush, and sits in an arena that resembles an outdoor auditorium with stage. The stream is the stage. Along the bank were spectators silently and politely observing the anglers; and in the water, roughly waist deep in the clear, nearly still flow of current backed by a small spillway, were the equally silent fishermen, respectfully spaced from each other, but filling the water nevertheless. I decided to watch.

It was an interesting thing to see. Each angler seemed to have a nearly flawless casting style, laying out crisp, controlled casts to visible, rising trout. I had never seen anything like it at home. So many fishermen, so many trout; the trout must surely have been as aware of the fishermen as the fishermen were of the trout. I was used to wild fish—fish who ran for cover at the merest hint of human intrusion. These trout seemed to know that they fed in the presence of peril, and they continued to do so, appearing to trust their ability to know a real insect from an artificial one.

This was a very strange kind of fishing indeed; it appeared challenging and difficult. To say that I was intimidated would be putting it mildly. Still, I had not come this far to simply watch. I walked upstream a bit, to a place with fewer anglers, no spectators, and a streamside wood to hide my less-than-perfect casting . . .

Aquatic entomology is the study of bizarre Latin names for common insects. When you use Latin, you give the fish the impression that you know as much as they do, so they'd better just give themselves up easy-like, because sooner or later, you're going to bore them to death with nomenclature anyway. I'll give you an example. On the Yellow Breeches, in the summer, an insect that hatches pretty reliably, and on which the trout seem to feed,

49

is a pale white mayfly, a couple of millimeters long (we amateur scientists always use the metric system; that bores the fish faster than the English system, which they understand), and it has a Latin name that means something like *Pale White Mayfly, A Couple of Millimeters Long*. For those of you who are serious about this, the fly is called the *Leukoboron gluteus maximus*, and if you mumble the Latin while you tie on a small white fly, you are doing what we anglers call Aquatic Entomology.

Anyway, an angler who knows his aquatic entomology will not just slip into the water and start flailing about with any old fly. What you do is, you take a small fine-mesh net, and you hold it in the current. You look at the incredible collection of mayflies, caddis flies, ants, beetles, midges, and pine needles that collect, and you file this information away. Then you get out a larger wire-rimmed net and you try to hold it on the bottom of the stream while you kick around in the rocks just upstream. You remove the net, and with your shirtsleeves dripping ice water down your armpits and into your waders, you examine what you have collected. You will probably find some yucky looking things called nymphs, maybe a few twigs and pebbles you'll want to call cased caddis (but won't be sure), and a lot of things that fall into other categories of existence beyond the class Insecta (you have no responsibility

to identify those). Again, you file this away.

After watching the fish feeding to determine whether they are taking flies from the surface, just below the surface, or down near the bottom of the stream, and after processing the massive amount of useful information you got when you soaked all that water into your shirt and felt it running to your crotch, you yell to the nearest angler, "Hey pal, what are you usin'?" You'll probably get lied to, but you tie it on if you have one, and off you go. Isn't science fun!

By the time I got into the water of the Yellow Breeches, I was pretty damn scared. I didn't know much about the insects on the stream, I knew my casting wouldn't be very pretty, and I was afraid that someone would correct my pronunciation if I tried to mumble something in Latin. Then I remembered two things that proved to be critical. First, I remembered a conversation I had with Barry Kustin, the genius who makes magnificent fly rods out of a combination of split bamboo and laminated graphite. We were admiring a rod he had built based on Vincent Marinaro's tapers, and we talked about the master. "Marinaro gave us a wealth of information in his books," he said, "but did you know that he almost always fished downstream?" No, I didn't, and it certainly wasn't obvious from his text that he

50

did. I also remembered an article by the late Ken Miyata, who argued that it is sometimes better to fish an imitation that isn't of the dominant insect during a large hatch, but one the trout are used to. He suggested an ant. I thought, why not a small caddis fly?

I tied on a #18 tan elk-hair caddis, a fly I use all the time at home, and one with which I feel quite comfortable (I suspect this is something like the feeling Ken had for ants). I didn't use any of the #20–#24 midges I had bought, nor that small white thing so popular on the Yellow Breeches. I fished the caddis imitation downstream, with a lot of slack in the long leader (like Vincent had), not up and across as everyone else was doing.

In about forty-five minutes I managed to raise,

strike, and land four nice fish. After the second or third, I noticed that I had gathered something of a crowd. Apparently, no one else had been having much luck that day.

When the fishing slowed down, as it did after a while, I climbed out of the water and enjoyed a wonderful conversation with some others who had been fishing near me. They asked me what I had been using and why I fished it the way I did. I avoided Latin, but in my best down-home Colorado accent (or at least what I thought they might interpret as down-home Colorado talk), I talked about "anting the hatch," or cadissing the hatch, as I had done. I spoke about my admiration for Vince Marinaro and his methods. I tried to represent all Colorado trout fishermen as sophisticated, successful anglers, who spoke slow but thought fast. I tried to do Colorado proud. And I must admit (get thee behind me, oh cursed pride) that I enjoyed their interest and respect.

If you are one of those kind and friendly fishermen who maybe remembers the Colorado angler with the beat-up red station wagon, the guy who caught all those brown trout and graciously shared the secrets of his success, the guy who had the scratched-up, old, eight-and-a-half-foot homemade graphite with the badly worn Pfleuger reel . . . if you remember the skinny guy with the black cowboy hat (only one in Pennsylvania, as far as I recall)—please don't read the rest of this. I want to continue basking in the glory of that moment. Truth requires, however, that I add the following.

I've gone back to Pennsylvania a few times since then, even fished at Allenberry. During my next trip, I slipped into the water closer to the spectators, not hidden by the trees, tied on my trusty #18 tan elk-hair caddis, and failed to interest a trout. Not only that, the old bastards swam over to me and laughed in my face! I sifted surface water for insects and soaked my shirtsleeves seining the bottom. Mumbling all the Latin I could remember, I frantically changed flies, trying to browbeat the trout into submission. This time, they saw me for what I was—a rube. Fortunately, I'd had my moment of glory, and no smartass Eastern trout would ever be able to take that away from me.

52

FISHING THE BEAVERKILL RIVER, NEW YORK BY KITTY PEARSON-VINCENT.

Some have described trout and salmon fishing as an obsession. I guess there is a fair degree of validity in the observation. Some collect tackle, others literature, still others collect both with an ardor that is unbelievable. We spend time fishing, talking about fishing, dreaming about fishing, and planning our future trips. The root of this behavior, however, is not material. We will never understand the desire to fish if we look for it in rods and reels, flies and fly boxes, or books and brochures. We will fail to find it as well if we only look at the act of fishing. Angling takes place in the world of the quiet wood, the thin air surrounding an alpine lake, the wide plain of the broad river. These places were our home before we invented tackle, long before we created books. Our obsession is, in many ways, a journey home.

Above: campsite, unnamed lake, Wind River Range, Wyoming by Tom Montgomery; right: Little Pigeon River, Smoky Mountains National Park, Tennessee by Willard Clay.

56

STORM CLOUDS GATHER OVER THE MADISON RIVER, MONTANA. PHOTOGRAPH BY KITTY PEARSON-VINCENT.

CASTING ABOUT

During a canoe trip to the Missouri Ozarks toward the end of my college days, I looked into the water of the Current River and saw living shadows darting for the cover of big rocks and undercut ledges. Something inside me wiggled.

A few years later after graduate school in Chicago (not many trout there I'm afraid), I moved to the mountains and was given a ''guided tour'' deep in the San Juan mountain country of southwestern Colorado. My guide was a wonderful man who was able to look back with pride at about sixty years in the San Juans. Jim was a mountain man, born and bred. His grandfather was one of the early prospectors who found gold here; he found enough, in fact, to begin the workings that have kept the San Juan County economy afloat for nearly a hundred years. But that's not all he found. He found trout too.

The love of trout and trout fishing is as much a part of this country as mining, and trout fever is as common in the old-timers as gold fever. Jim was no exception. We fished a lot during that memorable trip. I used a spinning rod, but Jim cast the fly. Watching him fish, something stirred in me again.

Shortly thereafter, I rediscovered angling and the fly rod, both distantly remembered from childhood days spent fishing with my father. My father was more hunter than angler, however, and my casting instruction had been limited. Stubborn and proud as I was though, I figured I was a pretty good caster and didn't need further instruction. How dull to begin fishing after we have had lessons from a qualified casting instructor. How boring to learn casting in a pond with edges free of bushes. How silly to begin an affair with fly rods and fly lines with a piece of yarn tied to the end of a short leader. Real streams, real flies, real fish! That's the way to learn. Right? Wrong.

During the first summer of my arrival in the mountains, and soon after my trip to the headwaters of the Rio Grande with Jim, I managed to assemble a fly-casting rig. That first outfit consisted of an eight-foot Fenwick fiberglass rod, a Pfleuger reel, and a double-tapered, six-weight line. I fished often and had a lot of fun with that gear. It was a nice setup and it served me well, but graphite was getting to be the thing, and I wanted a new rod. My casting was pretty poor, but I didn't know it. I was better than most I'd seen (I hadn't seen any really good fly-casters at that point), and I was able to catch fish. I particularly liked to fish a nearby lake which was wadeable out from shore to about thirty feet, where there was a shelf and a sudden drop. From the shelf to a weed bed where the big fish hung out, it was about seventy-five or eighty feet. Often I would try to catch those fish, but I just couldn't seem to get a fly to them. But with a graphite rod . . .

So I ordered one. Nine shiny feet of one. And a weight forward, fluorescent green, Rocket Taper line. I was certain that those lunkers would now be mine. The first evening I had the new rod, I didn't practice with it. I didn't tie on a piece of yarn and get the feel of it. It was barely out of the wrapper when I went lunker hunting.

With a #8-6XL, royal coachman bucktail clinch-knotted to the end of my leader, I drove up the mountain, walked to the lake, waded into position, stripped damn near the whole line off the reel and onto the water near my waders, and began to play out line. What a feeling. It was fantastic! I couldn't believe the line speed I was generating. I let out more and more line until I had the entire forward section out, and then I began to push hard, preparing to shoot fifty feet of running line out to the behemoths who hid in the watery garden. What excitement, what joy, what happiness! Happiness, that is, until the line that had been dropping steadily with each false cast zinged across my face on a backcast and hooked the dumbest behemoth in the lake firmly in the lip.

I cut the leader, leaving the fly in my rapidly swelling lip, gathered up my tackle and what was left of my pride, staggered from the water and drove home—fly dangling from my face.

I was greeted at the door with a voice from another room. "How did you like the new fly rod, honey?'' When Karen emerged through the doorway her eyes met mine, then scanned my lip. A gentle loving soul stood before me, not knowing whether to pout in sympathy or laugh hysterically. Her internal battle didn't last too long. She laughed hysterically.

Somewhere between the thwack of the fly into my face, my floundering exit from the lake, the drive home, my humiliating arrival, the pushing of the fly through my mouth, and the cutting off of the barb, I resolved two things. I was damn sure going to fish with barbless hooks for a while. And I was going to work on my casting.

Casting the fly rod is quite different from casting with spinning or bait-casting tackle, and the generally agreed on difficulty of learning to cast a fly with a long rod and a fat fly line is one of the reasons many fishermen never become fly-casters.

In casting a baited hook, or weighted lure, the weight at the end of the fishing line is what hauls the line out in the cast. The rod, in effect, throws a focused weight—the lure carries the line. In fly casting, however, the lure has very little weight and cannot generate the momentum required to haul a fishing line any distance. Instead, the weight is distributed over the length of a thick fly line, and the line then is accelerated by the rod—the line carries the lure.

Fly-casting is an elegant thing to watch, and it appears a good deal more complicated than other forms of casting. In truth, learning to fly-cast is actually no more difficult than learning to swing a golf club or a tennis racket. Though few wield fly rods brilliantly, almost anyone can learn to use one competently. The problem, I believe, lies in the fact that most fishermen are lazy—so they think a person should be able to pick up a fly rod, and cast. Unfortunately, that just doesn't work. A little practice is needed to learn the basics; more practice is needed to develop skill.

Having a good teacher around when you're getting started is nice, but in my experience, it is not too terribly common. Most of us learn from our fathers or friends (who are rarely qualified to teach), or we teach ourselves and pick up some pretty bad habits in the process.

These days I do most of my practicing in the winter when I can't fish and when I want to be connected to fishing in some way. Fact is, working on my casting has never seemed like a chore to me. I rather enjoy it. For many years I lived in a small mountain town where spring was always a long time coming. Often I would break the patterns of a long winter by casting on the snow-covered street in front of my house. Toward spring I would cast to the water-filled potholes that emerged from the snow-

59

pack. Not until years later, after many seasons of casting to the potholes, did the guy who lived across the street manage to screw up the courage to tell me that my neighbors thought I was nuts. When I asked why, he replied, "'Cause every damn spring we see you come out here tryin' to catch fish out of the damn potholes! Goshsake a'mighty, Steve, you haven't ever caught one yet, you haven't ever even *seen* one, why the hell do ya keep tryin'?" This was a town that understood cabin fever and spring madness, so I wasn't totally ostracized. But it didn't help my social standing, I'm sure.

A pond or lake is best for practicing, because the lifting of the line from water is an important part of casting. Some casts (the roll cast and Spey cast, for example) are impossible to practice properly without water. In the absence of water, a large lawn or park green will do.

Find a really good caster, or better yet a professional casting instructor, and get some pointers. It helps to know what a good cast looks like and what is good form. Imitating the styles found along the stream is not always wise.

For years I had noticed that good casters seem to have an amazingly distinct bump in the casting motion that appears in the rod as a quick snap. The part of the casting stroke (so obvious in the motion of such great casters as Steve Rajeff) that causes this is called different things by different people. Most often I've heard it called the "power-snap." Important to learn but a hard thing to teach, the power-snap depends on timing. It appears in the casting sequence after the "loading" motion. The total collection of movements that results in a cast is often described as "load-snap-wait (back), load-snap-wait (front)." If you snap too soon or too abruptly, the cast disintegrates, the line does a jig instead of a waltz, and the leader ties itself in knots. The loading motion, the snap, and the wait (which in better casters' motions includes a movement called drift) have to blend together into a sequence without separate parts—a motion with a smoothly flowing change of emphasis. Can you imagine how meaningless this language must seem to someone who has yet to feel a proper cast?

Reading and talking about casting, I fear, is a little like reading and talking about sex. Even with pictures, it just isn't the same. If you want to cast well, you have to forget the language. Forget the theory, and learn the *feeling* of casting. Giving you a feel for the proper motion is what good instructors will do. Bad ones will talk theory. If you want to talk theory, fine. Do it later.

Not too long ago I watched Mel Krieger teach a group lesson at a sportsmen's exposition. What a lesson it was! I've been to comedy clubs where I

didn't laugh as often or as hard. He told jokes, he imitated typical fishermen, he told stories, and he cast. I saw casters who had never held a rod before, casting well enough to go fishing after a half hour. Experienced casters who had picked up some bad habits along the way lost them, and were casting with more control, distance, and accuracy.

Fly-fishing schools that offer excellent casting instruction are springing up everywhere. Many local chapters of Trout Unlimited and the Federation of Flyfishermen also offer casting classes. There is no need to thrash about in ignorance. Take it from one who knows, unless you like having fish hooks embedded in your face, that is, in which case you might be able to merge fly-fishing and the age-old profession of the fakir. Not that I'm knocking it, mind you. I got a lot of attention when I tried it.

61

62

Photograph by Kitty Pearson-Vincent.

Casting instruction is something every angler can benefit from, especially if the instructor is someone like Joan Salvato Wulff. A tournament casting champion, ardent angler, and superb instructor, Joan leaves her students with more than improved casting skills—somehow she manages to communicate her passion for life as well.

Photograph by Kitty Pearson-Vincent.

American angling has included a handful of legitimate legends, and Lee Wulff is one of them. Perhaps best known for his incredibly successful series of hairwing flies (the various Wulffs), Lee is known among serious anglers as a devoted conservationist who has worked long and hard to protect and preserve trout habitat, and to restore the former greatness of North American Atlantic salmon runs.

64

Snake River, Idaho by R. Valentine Atkinson/Frontiers.

Big water calls for special technique. On a big river, in swift current, there is no substitute for a boat.
The most popular angling craft, by far, on western water is the dory, usually called a drift boat.

Martis Lake, California by R. Valentine Atkinson/Frontiers.

This fine rainbow is the result of fishing from a platform that has become increasingly popular in the past few years. Known as belly boats, float tubes, or simply tubes, these lightweight craft are quite versatile, amazingly stable, and are an excellent compromise between the uncomplicated comfort but limited access of the wading angler, and the cumbersome paraphernalia but free-roaming capability of the boat fisherman.

66

There have been many summers when the lure of the high mountain lake was so strong that stream and river fishing were almost forgotten. Lake fishing can be quirky, and high lakes extremely so. Many a long, difficult hike to a lake that yielded countless trout on one trip has ended without trout on subsequent trips. But there are consolations—alpine flowers at your feet, eagles soaring overhead, deep blue skies during the day, alpenglow at dusk, and a night sky so full of stars the heavens appear white—all strong antidotes to any sadness from slow fishing.

Above: brook trout by Tom Montgomery; right: Ediza Lake, California by Larry Ulrich.

68

STEELHEAD, THOMPSON RIVER, BRITISH COLUMBIA BY KITTY PEARSON-VINCENT.

SEA RUNS

The steelhead is a mythical creature." This may be true, but I'm not the one who said it. On my way home from Campbell River after a Vancouver Island fishing trip, I stopped into Kaufmann's Streamborn in Portland to see this special fly shop whose catalogs I'd been reading for years. While there, I began to talk about my recently completed trip "up island," and mentioned that the steelhead I had gotten into seemed to be haunting me while I was awake, filling my sleep with vivid dreams, and dominating my thoughts in a way no fish ever had. The clerk, a veteran of many steelhead campaigns, winter and summer, just smiled. When I asked what his favorite game fish was he spoke reverently of trout and salmon, but his deepest respect, his most profound sense of wonder, is reserved for the steelhead. A magical fish, a mythical creature, he said.

The trout can be wary, and difficult. It can refuse an imitation you *know* is perfect, gently sipping a natural inches away from your fly. You might fish over a selective trout for hours, yet love every minute. A good trout can run into your backing, dance on the water when hooked, and fill you with admiration.

Salmon shine like silver in the glow of sea-seeking rivers. They are large and strong, often difficult to catch on a fly in fresh water, and feel awesome at the end of a leader—their heartstopping runs or deep, brooding stubbornness when hooked feel like no other fish. But steelhead are something else, something else entirely.

When British and European-American anglers first discovered steelhead in the rivers of the Pacific coast (native Americans had, by this time, known them for centuries), the fish were a complete enigma. They seemed to be trout, they lived like salmon, and they had a power and speed never before seen in a troutlike fish. The early writers said steelhead could not be caught on conventional tackle: lines would snap like thread; rods would splinter under the strain; lightning runs, with broad-sided bodies turning into the heavy currents of western coastal rivers, would cause fish to disappear as magically as they had appeared, leaving both dreams and tackle shattered. This prediction, like others of the early explorers, proved untrue. Steelhead were eventually caught on conventional tackle, and today they are routinely caught with bait rods and spinning tackle, and on the deeply drifted wet fly and the dry fly. This is not to say that the steelhead is any less mysterious, or has lost any of its incredible hold on the angler's imagination.

Part of the mystery of the steelhead has been solved by science. This trout, which seems so like a salmon, is, in fact, a rainbow trout, but one that leaves the confines of its spawning gravel and the limited waters of the river where it was born for the sea's greater variety and abundance of food. Like salmon, they grow to massive size in the salt water

and acquire incredible power. When they return to their home streams to spawn, they are nothing like the landlocked trout inhabiting interior streams and lakes. Discovering that steelhead are actually rainbows was a major step in understanding their biology, but many questions remain. We still know little of their migratory ranges or their behavior at sea.

Picture a strong wide river running to the sea. A salmon run is building, and in the broad water of flood tide, not far above the estuary where fresh water meets the salt, the pinks are surfacing everywhere. Occasionally the loud crash of an early Chinook, broaching like a whale, can be heard from the deep run on the far side of the river. It is late afternoon in early August. The cloudy sky softens the light and makes the world glow. A pair of bald eagles is circling above. Gulls come in waves, and go. This is the Campbell River, Vancouver Island, British Columbia.

My son and I had just arrived. We were staying at the Campbell River Lodge and Fishing Resort, where saltwater guides are forever arriving with happy clients who have taken Chinooks in the twenty-pound class, Coho around ten pounds, and the occasional cod from the fertile waters of the Straights of Georgia. Our plan was to settle in, get oriented, and head up the Campbell the next day to fish, but the sight of all those pinks rising, the sound of the Chinooks crashing, and the beauty of the river were too much—I couldn't wait. Daniel watched the guides clean salmon, the gulls squabble over the scattered debris discarded into the tidal flat beyond the lawn, and the ritual of weighing and photographing big Chinooks, while I donned my waders and rigged my salmon and steelhead rod. I walked out into the river, directly in front of our hotel room, and began to cast.

The Campbell has few steelhead in the summer, but there are enough to make it possible to get into one. I fished a sinking line in the fast current, mended it to give the fly time to search the bottom, held it in the current at the end of its swing, stripped in some line, and finally cast again.

The first strike came at the end of a swing, and compared to those I had been getting from Colorado trout, it was quite strong. A well-hooked fish took off directly across the river and ran about sixty feet before stopping. I recovered the backing that was out and a good bit of line before the fish ran again, my reel singing a sweet, shrill song. But steady pressure against the exposed rim of the reel spool halted this run too. It became easy to hold the fish, easy to recover line, and after a few minutes of short runs and slow circling, I netted a big, wonderfully shiny, fresh pink salmon of about six pounds. The fight lasted close to seven minutes. A few more minutes were needed to revive the fish and send it on its way.

This scenario repeated itself many times and was quite a thrill. These were strong, fresh pinks—clean and bright. Their sides, though predominantly silver, carried a delicate red sheen that seemed luminous. Their bodies were full and deep, their heads small. I began to get used to the take at the end of the swing, the long run, the short run, the circling and final struggle, and the ultimate surrender to the net—when something very different happened.

In the middle of a deep fly drift, I saw the line twitch where it entered the water. I lifted the rod. The ten feet of loose line in the water near me, line I was planning to use in the mending, ran through the stripping guide in an eye blink. Line began to knife through the water as if it were being towed by a hydroplane, and I watched as the line on my reel, and then my backing, disappeared at a pace that was hard to believe.

The pressure I applied to the spool, the same pressure I had used to halt the hooked salmon, had no effect, other than burning my fingers, and line continued to disappear. Turning into the broad current, the fish gained speed and headed downstream. I pushed my palm onto the reel spool, but this too had no effect—I could do nothing to slow

71

72

that fish down. Just before the hundred yards of backing ran out, I grabbed the spool, felt my ten-pound tippet snap, and stood, line limp in the water, listening to my rapid breathing and feeling a rush of adrenaline more appropriate to a near-fatal accident than a recreational sport, and stared at the broken surface of the water. Steelhead.

That evening I was distracted and all night I was restless. When morning came I was on the river again searching for another steelhead. Tall trees on the opposite bank barely showed through the misty air. Sky and water merged. My first cast took a nice pink in shallow water. Again the long run, the short run, the circling, the net, the release. The fog lifted, revealing three large raccoons that waded the opposite bank, foraging. Gulls circled overhead. The pinks continued to come to the fly at the end of the swing, and again the swing was interrupted.

This time a shiny torpedo came out of the water, my #6 Babine Special hanging from the corner of his mouth. He took to the air, pranced across the surface of the river, ran upstream, then down. I applied more pressure than before and the knots held. He turned upstream, and I thought, "I'm going to land this guy." Suddenly he turned downstream, and ran at a rate impossible to follow. The fly came loose, and once more I stood in the river with a loose line. But at least I had seen him! Another steelhead.

That afternoon Daniel and I fished with a local, a man named Newfee. He was a transplant from Newfoundland who had gone, as he said, from one island to the other. He knew the holes and runs of the Campbell well, and he took us to good steelhead water.

One pool, near the union of the Campbell and the Quinsam, looked especially promising, and the three of us fished it. Daniel cast into the water of the pool's tail. Good water. Newfee took the middle water, but told me that the eddy line between the rapid current tongue at the head of the pool and the calm water of its near edge usually held steelhead. To cast successfully into this water, I was forced to wade through some pretty difficult currents and over large mossy boulders, until I found a reasonably secure platform in waist-deep water from which to cast.

Still fishing the sinking line, I lengthened my line with each cast to cover the water (walking downstream from my precarious perch was impossible), and in a few minutes a steelhead nailed my fly and shot into a fast run. I applied as much pressure to my reel as I dared, pressing hard with my palm. It worked. About halfway down the pool, the silver monster leaped into the air, leaped again, and turned upstream. Each time he jumped, I lowered the rod, hoping to prevent a breakoff, and my luck

73

held, as did the knots and the fly. After these acrobatics and the first few minutes, I was still fast to the fish. I took time to glance at Newfee and Daniel who were watching, as amazed and excited as I. Newfee whooped each time the fish came out of the water. Daniel just stared, his eyes wide with wonder.

This battle had no slack moments. Each time the fish changed direction, he ran. He never rested. He passed between me and the shore, coming within inches of my feet, and I got a very close, very good look, my fly hanging from his jaw, before he raced upstream one final time, turned downstream, and disappeared into the tail of the pool where the fly let go. Gone.

We fished a few more hours, covering the famous island pools so beautifully described by Roderick Haig-Brown in his many books. We saw two others fly-fishing, but saw no more steelhead. Newfee had a hookup with a good fish, again at the head of a pool, but his leader was broken in the early going, before the fish showed itself.

After the second fish, daylight began to fade. We collected our tackle and a few beers (judiciously stashed in the woods), walked back to the car in the dark, and swapped stories. Newfee's accent grew stronger, until even he admitted that sometimes his ''Newfanese'' got so thick his wife couldn't understand him. But he did say something I understood perfectly, and I can still hear him saying it: ''Boy, that was some fish you got into.'' Yes, it was.

I've spoken with a fair number of steelheaders since then, and they all agree—I can count that fish, the one that swam past my feet. I never held him in my hands. I didn't revive and release him, but for a steelhead . . . ''You saw him at your feet? Hell, that one counts!''

Here, the nearest steelhead stream is about seven-hundred miles away, but I find myself dreaming the same dreams I dreamed when I slept on the banks of the Campbell. I had heard it before, but never knew how true it really is: Once you've been into a steelhead, you're never the same. And I'll tell you one more thing. It won't be too long before I'm back on that beautiful island casting a fly for those magnificent fish. Chill me a beer, Newfee. I'm as good as there.

74

MIGRATING RED OR SOCKEYE SALMON, LAKE CLARK TRIBUTARY, ALASKA BY JIM BRANDENBURG.

76

King salmon, Alaska Peninsula by R. Valentine Atkinson/Frontiers.

For all but the few lucky local anglers, a trip into Alaska involves a lengthy journey. The rewards, however, are tremendous. Pristine wilderness of staggering scale provides spawning water for huge populations of sea-run and resident fish. Salmon and steelhead that return to Alaska grow to immense proportions. Fifty-pound Chinooks are routinely caught from Alaskan waters, and fish approaching a hundred pounds are possible.

Sustut River, British Columbia by Jim Vincent.

Each steelhead in the net is usually the result of many hours on the stream. This is one of the differences between steelheading and trout fishing. During a good rise, the competent fisherman usually strikes, plays, and lands many fish, but steelhead, more often than not, come to the fly less often. Perhaps this is why each steelhead is remembered.

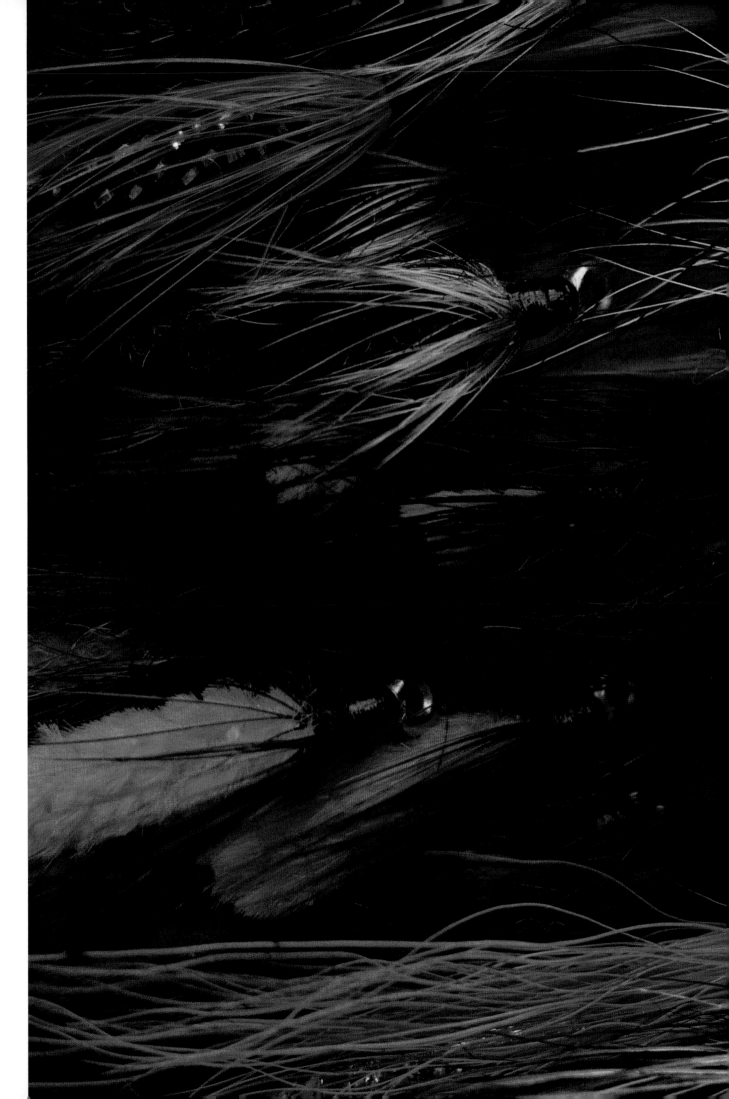

After the drab, imitative flies that dominate
trout fishing, steelhead and salmon flies come as a
bit of a shock. Steelhead are known to feed in fresh
water, but they do not feed as readily or as often
as stream-resident fish. The questions of whether
and how salmon feed in fresh water have not been
resolved. Consequently, steelhead and salmon flies
are designed to appeal to instincts similar to, but
not the same as, those that guide feeding. Gaudy,
fluorescent colors dominate many of the newer
patterns. Traditional salmon flies are usually a bit
less showy, but are colorful nonetheless. The
traditional, fully dressed salmon fly is without
question the most elegant of flies. It is also the
epitome of the fly-dresser's craft.

Above and right by Tom Montgomery.

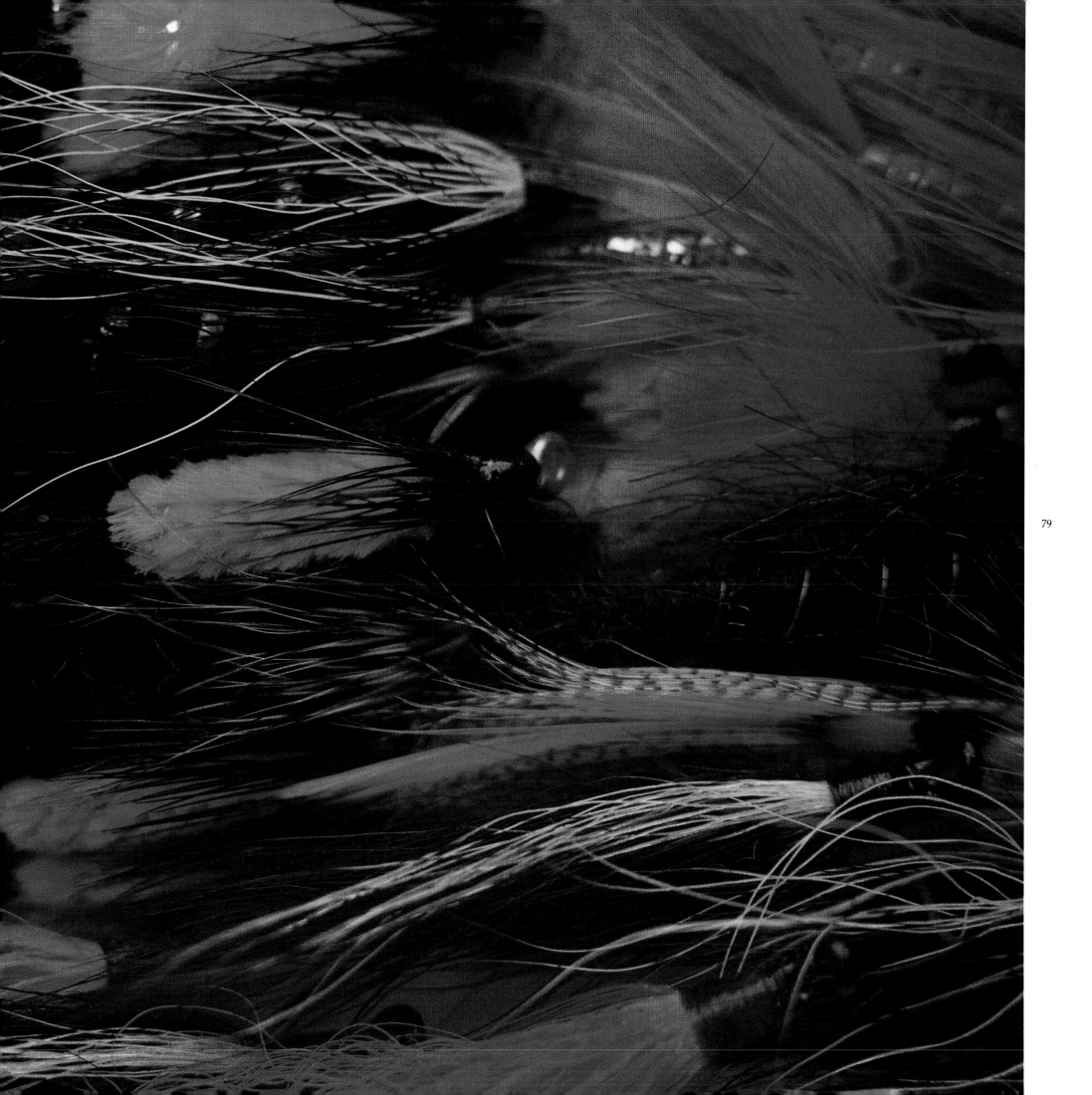

80

Enchanted Lake, Katmai National Park, Alaska by R. Valentine Atkinson/Frontiers.

Alaskan fishing is often remote fishing. Much of the guided angling in Alaska is done after float-plane flights to wilderness rivers and lakes. These distant waters are home to the big, wild fish that we all dream of, but rarely encounter.

Brooks River, Alaska by R. Valentine Atkinson/Frontiers.

Anglers are not the only creatures interested in salmon. Spawning salmon are a favorite food of the grizzly. More than one angler has vacated a prime fishing location to make room for one of these Alaskan fishermen.

81

82

DOCUMENTING THE EVIDENCE, HAT CREEK, CALIFORNIA BY R. VALENTINE ATKINSON/FRONTIERS.

FISHING STORIES AND THE NATURE OF TRUTH

Fishermen aren't liars, exactly; but truth seems to mean something very different to a storyteller than it does to someone else. Fishermen, I believe, are the consummate storytellers. To approach fishing stories (and those who tell them) with an attitude completely unlike the one you'd bring to the evening news is probably wise. The following story demonstrates why.

I know that Colorado's Blue Mesa Reservoir is the home of some very large trout and landlocked salmon, so a few years ago I embarked on a journey up the Lake Fork arm of the reservoir. I canoed quietly through the glassy water, edging ever closer to my destination—a small inlet where I hoped the kokanee would be feeding.

Kokanee are difficult to take with the fly. The reason is simple: they feed on plankton, not flies. Their flesh is red and firm, and their flavor is exquisite; I wanted to take two for breakfast. I knew a method for catching them, and I was determined to prove its effectiveness. As the sun moved slowly toward the horizon, the sky grew red, as red as the flesh inside the shiny salmon that began to feed, sluggishly at first, and then with increasing frenzy, in the surface water of the bay.

A novice might have thought (wrongly) that they were feeding on midges, for their rise-forms looked much like those of smutting trout. Knowing them to be kokanee, however, I was neither fooled nor intimidated. I knew they'd defend their feeding lanes against intruders, so I devised a most fiendish ruse. I would assault their territory in the form of a small fish—a fish they would attack. Inside of the intruder would be a surprise. The small fish, you see, was not a fish at all, but an imitation, cleverly designed to goad the territorial kokanee into striking.

I paddled into position and gently pulled my "fish" through the feeding salmon, knowing that a strike would come. Every nerve firing, tense in anticipation, I awaited the first savage strike. When it came, its ferocity was unbelievable. A mammoth fish had taken the fly and raced off to deep water. Though played brilliantly, the salmon's strength overcame that of the tackle, and I nearly wept when, one complete fly line and nearly a hundred yards of backing gone, the tippet broke and the line went slack. No one will ever be able to convince me that the salmon I had hooked was not a world record.

Undaunted, I continued to fish. Soon I had another strike. This fish too fought valiantly, but the tippet held. When finally I netted the eighteen-inch monster, I knew I'd discovered the solution to the "plankton hatch." I angled confidently for another, wanting the brace to prepare for breakfast. In good time, another was led to the net. As the last remaining glow of dusk faded from the evening sky, I turned and paddled for camp, confident that the method, now tested and proven, would stay with me forever.

The truth is, a few years back I went on a canoe trip up a side canyon of Blue Mesa Reservoir. Fish were rising all over, which I thought were surface-feeding trout. I also thought that the rise-forms (and absence of visible insects on the water) indicated that they were rising to midges. I tied a #20 black midge on my tippet, caught nothing, got frustrated, and started changing flies. I tried small midge pupae in the surface film, then below the film. Nothing. I tried trusty old attractors, like the Royal Wulff, in several sizes. Nothing. Finally, in desperation, I tried stripping a gaudy Matuka streamer through the rising fish, hoping they would strike, if not from a desire for food, perhaps out of anger. Still nothing.

Trailing the gaudy streamer behind me, I began to paddle for shore, slowly at first, and then as fast as I could manage, partly to relieve the frustration, and partly for the simple joy of working hard against the paddle. To my complete surprise, a fish hit the streamer, the hook set itself, and I watched as line and then backing ran from the reel with incredible speed. I reached for the rod, accidentally snubbing the line against the grip, and felt the tippet snap immediately—one hour, one strike, and one fish lost to ham-handedness and stupidity. But at least I had found a way to get a strike.

I trolled at speed with the Matuka again and got

84

85

another strike. This time I jammed the paddle to halt the canoe and backpaddled in the direction of the fish before picking up the rod. Still the line ran from the reel, but in the deep, unobstructed water of this lake, even an idiot can hold a running fish, and I did. When finally he was landed, I discovered that my "trout" was a salmon—a very shiny fourteen-inch kokanee.

The skimming streamer worked on the kokanee, but I'd be hard pressed to say why. Perhaps it triggered a territorial defense or some other aggressive response. The strike it induced was largely random, and more a matter of luck than skill. I trolled for another and caught it. Having two salmon in the canoe, and knowing that breakfast would be an incredible feast, I paddled for camp.

A good fish story must have some connection to fact, but the connection must be flexible. If the day is ordinary, it must be painted with more exotic colors. The water is either glassy or raging, never simply smooth or flowing. The fish must always be heroic and huge. Mistakes are never made. Fishermen are done in only by the cunning tactics of their quarry, the violence of the weather, or the limitations of their tackle.

When I was a child, I would listen with wide eyes to the tales my father and his friends would tell. The stories I remember best are those he and his best friend Jack would weave in front of Jack's fireplace, as I sat on the floor hugging Betsy, Jack's faithful old hound dog. Both Jack and my dad worked part-time for the Department of Fish and Game as deputy

Dolly Varden, Agulawak River, Alaska by Jim Vincent.

A fine fish like this one can make the day for a young angler—heck, it can make a summer. But catching a big fish is more than a momentary experience; it is the start of a collection of tales. We begin our personal collections, our individual mythologies, with our first fish. For many, the stories begin with the first trout. Still others believe it begins when our first trout is taken on a fly.

WITH THIS ATLANTIC SALMON, THERE IS NO NEED FOR EXAGGERATION, GAULA RIVER, NORWAY BY R. VALENTINE ATKINSON/FRONTIERS.

wardens during hunting season. Their best stories involved observations they had made while on duty, of hunters being outfoxed by fox, deer, bear, you name it. The animals in these tales always won, and they were always wiser than the hunters. These stories invariably began with the words, "And they call 'em dumb animals!" The stories ended with these words as well.

Later in the evening, by the time they'd had a few shots of Scotch and a good many hearty laughs, they'd start to tell their own hunting and fishing stories; however, in these stories, although the prey were always worthy, noble, and wise, they rarely escaped. In the end, the deer and bear were shot. The trout landed. Or on the rare occasion that an animal did manage to escape, it left behind a precious piece of information in the process. It never dawned on me that there was an inconsistency here.

Years later, as I too became old enough to sit around after an adventure and retell the tale with friends, I found that the experience I heard recounted in the bar or living room was never quite the same as the one I had experienced in the woods, on the mountain, or in the stream. I also learned that these stories were infinitely more interesting to non-participants than anything as mundane as simple, unembellished truth.

For a good many years I climbed and hiked with a couple of friends. One of these friends lived here in the mountains year-round, but the other left each autumn to make a living in Baltimore. All winter long the two of us who remained told the stories of our summer adventures together. In the spring, when J.P. rejoined us from Baltimore for another summer in the mountains, we would go out to a bar together and tell the stories again. Somewhere in the middle of a story, it would dawn on J.P. that we were talking about a trip in which he had participated. It always amazed him how much more interesting the stories had become in his absence.

This is the nature of storytelling, but what is the nature of truth? Let me rephrase that. What is the nature of Truth? Truth with a small *t* is accuracy. Truth with a capital *T* is meaning. Truth with a small *t* is what happened. Truth with a capital *T* is why we were there when it did. So I always divide the number of fish caught in a story by 1.5 if I want truth, but listen with my heart when I want Truth.

I love a fishing story, full of cliches, exaggerations, and raging or glassy water, and I never contradict a fellow angler when he is telling a story (*Moby Dick* moves us so much more than *The World Almanac*). And this is why I laugh when friends ask me why I don't write more fiction. How could I? I already write fishing stories.

86

another strike. This time I jammed the paddle to halt the canoe and backpaddled in the direction of the fish before picking up the rod. Still the line ran from the reel, but in the deep, unobstructed water of this lake, even an idiot can hold a running fish, and I did. When finally he was landed, I discovered that my "trout" was a salmon—a very shiny fourteen-inch kokanee.

The skimming streamer worked on the kokanee, but I'd be hard pressed to say why. Perhaps it triggered a territorial defense or some other aggressive response. The strike it induced was largely random, and more a matter of luck than skill. I trolled for another and caught it. Having two salmon in the canoe, and knowing that breakfast would be an incredible feast, I paddled for camp.

A good fish story must have some connection to fact, but the connection must be flexible. If the day is ordinary, it must be painted with more exotic colors. The water is either glassy or raging, never simply smooth or flowing. The fish must always be heroic and huge. Mistakes are never made. Fishermen are done in only by the cunning tactics of their quarry, the violence of the weather, or the limitations of their tackle.

When I was a child, I would listen with wide eyes to the tales my father and his friends would tell. The stories I remember best are those he and his best friend Jack would weave in front of Jack's fireplace, as I sat on the floor hugging Betsy, Jack's faithful old hound dog. Both Jack and my dad worked part-time for the Department of Fish and Game as deputy

Trophy from Rock Creek, Montana by Donna Ulrich.

This winsome angler is celebrating a significant event in her young life. One's first fish, no matter how big, is always special, and the memory of that experience will always be as pleasurable as this youngster's smile.

90

Beautiful surroundings and extraordinary events make for vivid memories, but there are other reasons for an angler's remembrances. To fish we must look attentively; in the act of so perceiving we see many things we would ordinarily miss. Perhaps the most wonderful and surprising benefit of angling is the renewed freshness of vision we carry from the trout stream to our ordinary daily activities.

Above: Gibbon River, Yellowstone National Park, Wyoming by R. Valentine Atkinson/Frontiers; right: Little Redfish Lake, Idaho by Jeff Gnass.

92

Naknek River, Alaska by R. Valentine Atkinson/Frontiers.

One of the joys of Alaska is the variety of life found there. Relatively scarce in the Lower Forty-eight, grayling thrive in Alaska.

93

Alagnak River, Alaska by Terry Ring.

The grayling's glory is its dorsal fin. This fin, much larger on the grayling than any related fish, waves in the current like a multicolored flag. The iridescent colors, however, fade rapidly when a grayling is removed from the water.

94

RAINBOW ABOVE, MAYBE RAINBOW BELOW. ROCK CREEK, MONTANA BY LARRY ULRICH.

A SHORT DISCOURSE ON METHOD

René Descartes believed that of all the natural resources, common sense is the most widely distributed. And I believe that of all natural resources, trout are one of the least widely distributed. Given my experience (especially in early-season high water or if anyone happens to be watching me fish) or given a friend from somewhere else who is tired of hearing me brag about how great the fishing is and, I can tell you, trout are as scarce as Einsteinium.

Put together the commonality of common sense and the scarcity of trout when you really want to see one and you've got reason to believe that we would find some reliable methods for catching trout. This is, indeed, what has occurred.

Some techniques—the dead drift dry fly, the upstream nymph, the Leisenring lift, the induced take, the greased line and the "sudden inch"—are too well known and widely discussed in the literature to bear repeating here. What I'm going to talk about are the techniques we real anglers use to find and catch fish—the secrets of the trade. (Now I know one never reveals a favorite fishing hole unless a promise that the location will never be shared is extracted and sealed with blood; likewise, the true secrets of angling success aren't given away. Fishing, too, has its high priests; arcane knowledge is hoarded. Well, I think it's about time this wisdom is spread around.)

One useful technique is the nymph fished with lead on the tippet. A bright strike indicator is placed on the leader so that any subtle mouthing of the fly will be visible. Watching the indicator, the angler sets the hook whenever its motion appears abnormal. Unfortunately the motion is made to appear abnormal by any number of things: flowing water (an all-too-common problem on trout streams), wind, weeds, or the fly or lead hitting bottom. In fact, the indicator as normally fished is practically useless. *Real* nymph fishermen sense a take and set the hook on faith, mystically perceiving the strike. The indicator has nothing to do with seeing the take. Its usefulness lies elsewhere.

Follow, if you can, this particularly brilliant and subtle use of the strike indicator in a method I call the Tethered Tippet:

I often fish with nymphs and a weighted leader, and I frequently use some kind of strike indicator. I don't especially like to fish this way, but there's no doubting its effectiveness. Just the other day I discovered a new way to use this rig.

My fly was a golden stonefly nymph, and my leader was about ten feet long with two BBs crimped near the tippet knot about two feet above the fly. I was fishing this way because the water on the Dolores was awfully murky and the level was dropping rapidly from 1200 to 100 cubic feet per minute (the reasons for water releases, by the way, are as mysterious as any branch of arcane knowledge). The fish, as they say, were off their feed.

At one point, in a particularly heavy current, I saw my strike indicator disappear below the surface. Hoping it might be a trout, but suspecting otherwise, I tightened the line and felt a heavy weight against my rod. It was the healthy throb of the current pushing on a line that had bellied because the lead weights had found a home in the bottom. I freed the leader and began to gather in line to see whether my lead was still in place, and my fly still connected, when I felt a different kind of throb, a different heavy weight from the one I felt moments before. There was a fish on!

The fly, dancing at the end of the two-foot tippet anchored to the bottom, had managed to find the dumbest trout in the river. This trout must have hooked himself while I was freeing the line, and when I dislodged the weights I was fast to a fish. The trout, by the way, went about seventeen inches, was a brown (shall we reevaluate the myth of the brilliant brown trout?) and was the only fish of any kind I was able to hook all day.

(Those of you who have fished with downriggers on the Great Lakes already know the basics of this technique. I suggest you give it a try next time you're out stream fishing.)

Late in the day I ran into another fisherman who had caught "two good-sized browns!" When I asked what he'd been using he showed me his rig,

which was an eight-weight rod, casting (I use the term advisedly) a shooting head backed with monofilament running line. About eight feet down the leader he had placed three huge split shot, and at the end of an eighteen-inch tippet he had tied a #6 Montana nymph. No doubt he too had been fishing the Tethered Tippet method.

I'll recapitulate for those of you who weren't taking notes. First, place a strike indicator at the end of your fly line. It doesn't matter whether it floats or not. Put enough lead on your leader/tippet knot to take your line to the bottom quickly. Fish a big, ugly nymph of some kind. Watch your strike indicator like a hawk. When it goes down, and stays down, pull on your line to see that it is well stuck. Walk up and down the stream, pulling on your line until the lead frees itself. If you've done everything properly, a large brown trout will be connected to your fly.

I'd like to get into some other advanced techniques (like the Badly Dragging Wet Fly or the Totally Drowned and Sinking Dry Fly), but I'm afraid the elite clique of anglers to which I belong, those who use these methods often, would drum me out of the corps. But then, if Descartes were correct, most of you already know and use these methods; it's just your humility that keeps you silent.

97

98

Photograph by Tom Montgomery.

During profuse hatches and spinner falls, the number of insects on the water can be staggering. Mayflies, such as these Grey Drake Spinners often cover the surface of the stream. It is an exquisite agony to watch as a feeding trout rises toward your artificial, only to take a natural floating inches away.

Photograph by Kitty Pearson-Vincent.

If you see intense concentration coupled with more than just a little bit of whimsy in these eyes, you are correct. This caster is Mel Krieger, an extraordinary caster, a superb instructor, and one of the funniest men I have ever met. I sometimes wonder if he catches trout with his pinpoint casting, or just grabs them while they're laughing.

100

Smith River, Montana by Tom Montgomery.

The decision whether to fish alone or with friends is a personal one. Most of us vary our habits, sometimes fishing alone, sometimes with a single good friend or a group of friends. The pleasure of angling camaraderie is undeniable, and it is a lonely angler who always fishes alone.

Silver Creek, Idaho by Kitty Pearson-Vincent.

The pleasures of solitude and aloneness, when we choose to fish alone, are also undeniable. Solitude often allows keener perception. Solitude also breeds the introspection that frames our angling days with meaning.

102

Trouting has its universals, those things that remain constant with time and place, but a good deal of the charm of angling lies in regional differences. Techniques, tackle, and fly preferences vary as much as accents. A fisherman from Maine will likely look as different from a Wyoming angler as he sounds. Cultural historians are forever finding the roots of these differences in ethnic migrations; those of us who spend time outdoors, however, know they have more to do with the character of the land that surrounds us. The hills of Virginia are not the mountains of Alaska. A Colorado autumn is nothing like fall in New England. The scale of our topography, the variety and color of our woods, the size and character of our streams and lakes shape us as much as they shape the land. And they shape the way we fish as well.

Above: Mattawamkeag River, Maine by Willard Clay; right: Pemigewasset River, New Hampshire by Willard Clay.

104

SNOW FORMS A HEAVY CRUST ON BANKS OF THE SNAKE RIVER, ONTARIO STATE PARK, OREGON. PHOTOGRAPH BY WILLARD CLAY.

SEASONS AND RITUALS

Have you ever gone fishing in the middle of winter in trout country? It resembles the shimmering, angling days of summer or the amber days spent astream in the fall about as much as a hard-boiled egg resembles a Denver omelet.

For the most part, for most anglers, winter is not a time to fish; neither is it a time when trout are forgotten altogether. This is the time when the good fishing book is savored, when equipment is sorted, cleaned, repaired—then sorted, cleaned, and repaired again. It is a time for practice casting. It is the time when journal entries are read and reread, when days spent knee-deep in the water of a favorite stream are relived, and the next trout fishing season is anticipated with a long-ing that is difficult to describe.

Winter is also a time for tying flies. I'm not sure how many fishermen tie their own flies, but I feel sorry for those who don't. Not that I buy all that crap about not being a *real* angler unless you do. I'm not convinced that all the experimenting we do with patterns actually yields much in the way of benefits. Most of us seem to fish a handful of traditional patterns most of the time. I don't even believe that the average tyer can tie better flies than he can buy. Every good fly shop carries locally tied flies, which are beautifully crafted. The real reason for tying flies is to make it through the winter. All of that nonsense about pragmatic benefits aside, fly-tying is really nothing more than sublimation. It substitutes for fishing when fishing is impossible.

When I tie flies, I can imagine the fly on a leader, the leader on a line, the line floating in the currents of a favorite stream, and a lunker trout lying in ambush, waiting to pounce upon my clever deception. Maybe one of the reasons my flies never look quite as good as they might, is the fact that my mind is always somewhere else when I'm tying them.

This also explains why every winter, without fail, I repeat the same insane process, go through the same crazy motions, and never learn from experience. In the first weeks of winter I replace my most often used flies. The rest of the winter I tie bizarre creations I sincerely believe have the attractive power to launch me into stardom—the fly-fishing hall of fame. Greenwell's Glory, Sawyer's Pheasant Tail, Gordon's Quill Gordon, Hewitt's Bi-visible, Marinaro's Jassid, Wulff's Royal Wulff, Schwiebert's Letort Hopper. Meyers' KB Baby Bucktail? How about the House Mouse Nymph? The Gold and Red Killer-Diller?

Fortunately—with or without all the books, the equipment fondling, the long evenings of blank stares (behind which lurk the visions of streams past and future), the journal entries read and re-read, and the flies tied—the laws of nature provide for a wondrous phenomenon: spring follows winter. In this, on a long, cold and dreary winter's eve, we may find comfort.

Where I live, the progression from winter to spring is sometimes orderly, but more often than not late winter and early spring blend together interminably. Some years spring appears in May with a gradual warming, the melting of snow from the areas below timberline, the emergence of early shoots from the ground and people from their homes; buds appear on the cottonwood and aspen. Plants blossom and grow steadily into summer as May passes and June begins. But it doesn't happen this way very often. Warm days usually appear in January, making one wonder whether there will be an early spring; and they continue to appear, off and on through June, with increasing regularity. Between the warm days, the sprouting plants, and the early trickles of snowmelt are frigid days, often weeks of them without let up, days of snow and icy wind. Winter days—days that continue to appear until winter/spring ends abruptly and a full-blown summer emerges.

Then there's the issue of elevation to further confuse things. Spring may well arrive at 8,000 feet while it's still winter at 10,000. A day may begin in spring and quickly retreat back to winter as one hikes up high-country slopes to chase trout. Finally we've got microclimates to deal with. A sheltered nook on a south-facing slope at 10,000 feet might be springlike in April, while a north-facing gully at the same elevation sits firmly in the grasp of winter (and will continue to do so well into August).

Spring in the high country isn't so much a time of year (it just can't be so neatly identified) as it is a state of mind. Spring, as a state of mind, always means fishing, whether the fish are ready or not.

One of the nice things about the delay between spring above timberline and spring in the valleys is the fact that there are days when the water flows, insects hatch, and fish are active before the high altitude snowmelt runoff begins. Some years this period lasts for weeks, and in those weeks the valley fishing is often excellent.

But sooner or later, big fish, warm weather, and the lure of valley fishing are not enough. I feel the need to find out whether my home waters are freeing up, whether my home fish are still there, which takes me to snow, ice-covered rocks, and the small but beautiful trout of Lime Creek and my favorite early season beaver pond along South Mineral Creek.

People think I'm crazy to admit that I fish these places as early as April (especially those who have been there). In April the lakes are still frozen solid, and in most years the streams are still covered with a deep blanket of snow. But this year was different. A mild winter and the early melting of a good deal of snow below timberline made the streams accessible far earlier than usual. A spring fishing trip was almost reasonable. Reasonability, however, was not the issue. I really had no choice. It is madness, but I am wonderfully locked in a dance step with these places and these fish. No matter that I have fished some during the winter, or angled the valley rivers in the lower altitude spring, my obsessive ritual continues with the high-country spring—whenever the water has opened up sufficiently to make casting a fly possible. I always explore the same places. I always cast the same flies. And I am always happy to see that the fish are still there.

I don't know why these two locations—upper Lime Creek and the beaver pond along South Mineral Creek—have become so important to me, but reasons immediately suggest themselves. Upper Lime Creek is home to a population of cutthroat trout that shows little sign of hybridization with other species, and is, therefore something of a rarity (a connection with a distant past when cutthroat were the only trout this country knew); the beaver pond holds a population of large brook trout that disappear in the summer, finding their way into the creek after the silt-laden, snowmelt-swollen waters have subsided. It is reliable early-season water. But these reasons are not sufficient to explain the nearly mystical attraction these two places seem to have. The reasons lie somewhere deep within me, buried in the relationship between me and this place I call home. This year, I managed to fish them both in one day, and to find trout in each place.

Early morning found me working my way up the streambed of Lime Creek near timberline, pulling my legs through streamside willows whose lower branches were still covered with ice that had formed during the night. I walked slowly, watching for trout, but saw none in the icy water. After about a half mile of wading, I came to a pool formed under a waterfall that tumbles down a stone cliff. The water's course is divided and spread as it falls, then gathered together again in the pool. The pool is a place where fish hold throughout the year, and I have never found it devoid of trout.

The first cast of a KB Special brought a strike, but the hook wasn't well set, and I lost the fish before I could land it. (This fly is one of those midwinter experiments that actually catches fish and has remained in my fly box; it is what the English might call a fancy fly, and is a tailless, wingless wet fly with a gold-ribbed cinnamon body that has a palmered brown hackle wound over it, and a brown, wet-fly-style hackle tied in at the red head. Mountain cutthroat seem to love it. And as long as we're speaking parenthetically, I'd like to add that this gaudy little number is no less ridiculous to look at than the countless others I have "invented," which don't

work worth a damn.) The second cast into the pool also brought a strike, and the fish, this time landed, was held and admired before being released. A few more casts brought a third fish to the fly. These trout were all small, jeweled beauties, with large spots. Some were brilliant red with electric blue halos or black ones, mostly concentrated on the rear of the body and above the lateral line. Each had a deep red gash on both sides of its throat. Small. Precious. Still alive after the long winter.

After the third fish, I turned and hiked back down the streambed. I ate a snack and drove to the ford on South Mineral Creek where I parked, re-rigged, and set out to cross the stream.

The beaver pond here has been something of a personal favorite ever since the day, years ago, when I cast an exploratory line and came up with a fat, fourteen-inch brook trout. I had never before seen a fish this large in the Mineral Creek drainage and considered it something of a rarity until subsequent casts brought strikes from several others, all virtual twins of the first. Since that June day, I have often fished the ponds in the early spring, and always found these large brookies hiding from the high water of spring runoff. This spring was no exception. The brookies were there, and they took a slowly stripped squirrel tail just as they had many times before.

In the other ponds were surface-feeding trout, little fellows perhaps four or five inches in length, dozens of them. They scurried for cover when they saw me walking, their wakes on the water evidence of the life that teemed below the surface. This too I have seen before, each spring.

What is it that makes a behavior a ritual? When does a repeated behavior become something more than merely an act we have done more than once? I suspect it has more to do with the meaning of the act than the fact that the act is repeated.

I return to these places each year whenever the rhythm of nature allows it. I go when the snow is beginning to leave the high country, before that departure swells into the torrent that marks the full-bore gush of spring. I smell the damp soil that until recently had been frozen. I feel the warmth of the sun on my face, and the gentle breath of the first balmy winds. Each year I go, and each year these things happen. And each year the balmy days are mixed with dark blustery days, days of cold and snow; but it matters little now, because spring has begun.

Photograph by Jim Vincent.

Few tyers ever achieve the status of legends. Walt Dette is such a man. The Catskill-style dry fly was originated by Theodore Gordon, long before Walt became famous, but his dedication to excellence and the beauty of his flies have defined the style. His has been one of the truly significant American contributions to angling.

Photograph by Kitty Pearson-Vincent.

When friends look into my fly boxes, the uninitiated always respond to the stonefly patterns with disgust. I suppose that is a compliment of sorts. These insects, which grow to unusually large size in some rivers, are a mainstay for catching trout in fast, oxygenated water.

112

Babine River, British Columbia by Tom Montgomery.

The phrase, "Dress for success," takes on new meaning when applied to the winter steelheader.

Babine River, British Columbia by Tom Montgomery.

Fly-fishing for winter-run steelhead was once considered a low-percentage proposition. Many anglers hedged their bets, carrying both fly- and bait-casting tackle to the stream. Fly-fishing for steelhead has undergone a major technical revolution in the past few years, and angler success with the fly has climbed steadily. Many anglers who once thought it too difficult now fish for steelhead exclusively with the fly.

114

It takes a great deal of dedication to fish in the winter (many say it takes a great deal of craziness), but some fish require us to be out on the stream when it would be a lot more comfortable to be at home in front of the fire. Winter-run steelhead are among the most exciting trout to catch, but they are available only during the cold months. Cold wind and wet snow are common when winter runs are at their best. Many hours of casting and shivering are usually endured before one connects with a winter-run steelhead, but time and cold are both forgotten when a good fish is running at the end of a leader.

Above and right: Babine River, British Columbia by Tom Montgomery.

Bighorn River, Montana by Tom Montgomery.

Cold weather is not the sole province of the steelheader. Many trout remain active throughout the winter in the relatively warm water of spring creeks and tailwaters. Air temperature has little to do with trout behavior. If you can keep the ice out of your rod guides long enough to cast, you can fish.

116

Brown trout, Bighorn River, Montana by Tom Montgomery.

Like any other day spent fishing, a winter day is full of rewards for the angler. Streams are less crowded, and solitude easier to come by. The stark winter landscape has a beauty very different from the lush excess of summer. A good trout taken in winter is savored, perhaps more than the easier fish of summer.

118

BALD ROCK CANYON, FEATHER FALLS SCENIC AREA, MIDDLE FORK OF THE FEATHER RIVER, CALIFORNIA BY JEFF GNASS.

A COMPENDIUM OF FLY-FISHING

TROUT& SALMON

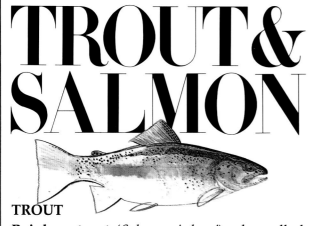

TROUT

Rainbow trout (*Salmo gairdneri*), also called rainbows, redsides, and bows, are native to the West Coast, although they have been distributed extensively by hatchery programs throughout the country. They are known particularly for their fighting qualities and the tendency to leap when hooked. Stream-resident varieties are often marked with a red band on the flanks, but rainbows found in large lakes often lack the red stripe making identification more difficult. Their backs, often colored in shades of brown or green, are usually darker than their bellies. Most stream-bred fish are also heavily spotted with small black speckles. The size range of rainbows can be tremendous—the largest caught by an angler went thirty-seven pounds, but far more common is the ten-inch hatchery rainbow.

Steelhead (*Salmo gairdneri*) are also known as steelies, and many local names apply to specific runs—springers, for example, are fresh, strong early arrivals to the Northwest. The steelhead is a rainbow that has migrated to the sea, fed on the ocean's bounty, and returned to the home stream to spawn. Steelhead are found in coastal rivers of the West and in interior states—rainbows that migrate into the

Great Lakes and return to their home streams to spawn are also considered steelhead.

Steelhead are bright in color when they arrive fresh from the sea, with backs darker than their silver sides. Like rainbows, they are spotted, but they lack the red stripe on their sides when they return. Male steelhead develop the stripe as spawning approaches.

Not all steelhead die after spawning, but few survive the rigors of spawning and return to the sea. Typical steelhead spend two years in salt water and range from five to ten pounds. Some steelhead approach twenty pounds. Although they are not commonly caught by anglers, steelhead of thirty and even forty pounds do occur.

Kamloops (*Salmo gairdneri gairdneri*) are a subspecies of rainbow native to the upper reaches of the Fraser, Columbia, and other rivers in British Columbia, with perhaps the most famous kamloops coming from Kootenay Lake. They have also been successfully stocked elsewhere.

The fame of these trout is based on several factors—the remoteness and beauty of their native range, their fighting qualities, and their good looks. But one factor distinguishes them from other trout: size. The average spawner in Kootenay Lake weighs ten pounds, but they can get much larger there, with twenty-five pounds being the upper limit.

California golden trout (*Salmo gairdneri aquabonita*) is one of several subspecies of golden trout, a term used to refer to several different fish (an Eastern char, the Sunapee trout, *Salvelinus alpinus oquassa*, is also called golden trout). California goldens are said, by most who have seen them, to be the most beautifully colored

of trout. The red band on their sides moves through a series of eleven oval parr marks (marks present on the juveniles of many trout and salmon, which usually disappear with maturity). Their backs are green, which fades to yellow-gold on the sides. Ventral fins are often brilliant orange, with pectoral and anal fins white-tipped and black-banded. Their backs and tails are spotted. The native range of California goldens is the upper Kern River drainage, but they have been stocked in many high altitude lakes and streams throughout the West. They tend to be small, averaging six to ten inches.

Brown trout (*Salmo trutta*), also known as brownies, German browns, and Loch Levans, are native to European waters where they exist in lake, stream, and sea-running forms. They were introduced in the U.S. in the 1880s, with original plantings coming from Germany and Scotland (hence the common names).

Browns are easily identified by their spots, which often include a mixture of black and red, with an occasional blue halo appearing. Backs tend to be brown or olive, changing to tan and yellow on the sides and bellies.

The size of browns varies greatly with location. Lake browns can grow quite large, up to thirty pounds, whereas many small streams sustain populations in the ten-inch class. Five-pound stream browns, however, are not rare.

Yellowstone cutthroat (*Salmo clarki bouvieri*). At last count there were fourteen subspecies of cutthroat trout. We choose the Yellowstone "cutt" as a representative because of its fame. Cutthroat are usually identified by the brilliant orange or red slashes on the throat. These marks, however, are not infallible

Rainbow, Silver Creek, Idaho by David Stoecklein.

guides. Cutthroat hybridize readily, and many rainbow-cutthroat hybrids (more rainbow than cutthroat) wear these marks.

Cutthroat are native to the West, and Yellowstone cutthroat are native to the Yellowstone region. Yellowstone cutthroat have large spots that cover the tail and decrease in number closer to the head. This fish is less brightly colored than other cutts. They have been distributed widely, but they probably achieve their greatest size in Yellowstone Lake, where they range from twelve to seventeen inches.

Coastal cutthroat (*Salmo clarki clarki*) are also known as cutts and bluebacks; they are often called sea-runs in anadromous form. Coastal cutthroat are native to the Pacific Coast rain forest that runs from southern Alaska to northern California. They exist in anadromous form, as well as in lake and large-river-dwelling varieties that spawn in tributaries. Also, there are stream-dwelling forms that do not migrate.

Sea-run fish are typically silver, with a yellow or brassy tint when they are fresh, and darken to look more like resident cutthroat, which have a pronounced brassy or coppery color. Coastal cutts have uniform spots with ventral fins that are occasionally yellow or red-orange. Throat slashes are usually visible, but can be faint in fish fresh from the sea. Coastal cutthroat are considered large at twenty inches.

Snake River cutthroat (unnamed, *Salmo clarki carmichaeli* has been suggested) is also known as the fine-spotted Snake River cutthroat and mountain trout. This trout was native to the waters of the upper Snake River in Wyoming, and has since been introduced into many other mountain waters of the West. Snake River cutts are distinguished from other cutthroat by the presence of small black spots, which are most densely concentrated on the rear of the fish and on the back, but spots are present on the sides and belly as well. Snake River cutthroat are typically ten to fourteen inches long, but can run to twenty-four inches.

SALMON

Chum (*Oncorhynchus keta*) are also called dog salmon. Chum salmon are native to the Pacific rim and populations occur in rivers from northern California to the Aleutians in Alaska. Runs in the Lower Forty-eight are small, with the only good-sized American runs appearing in Alaska. Chum resemble sockeye, but can be differentiated easily. Chum have a white-tipped anal fin and silver sides lacking spots but having faint gridlike bars. As spawning approaches, males develop severely hooked jaws with large canine teeth. Color darkens from the silver of fresh fish to an olive back, with maroon sides that have rust-colored bars. Typical chum weigh ten to fifteen pounds, but may go as high as thirty.

King (*Oncorhynchus tsawytscha*). King salmon have many names, Chinook, tyee, springs, and quinnat among them. The largest of Pacific salmon and the largest salmonid taken on the fly in North America, kings range from northern California to Alaska, with the largest runs and the biggest fish occurring in Alaska. Kings are distinguished from Coho, with which they can be confused, by their black gums and forked tail covered with spots. Kings can grow to over a hundred pounds. In California, Oregon, and Washington, they typically weigh twenty to thirty pounds; in Alaska, kings of fifty pounds are frequently caught by anglers.

Sockeye (*Oncorhynchus nerka*) are also known as red salmon and blueback salmon, and the landlocked form is the kokanee. Native to the Pacific rim, sockeye can be found as far south as the Sacramento River in California.

Sockeye are recognized by their large, glassy eyes. Spawning males develop startling colors, with brilliant red bodies and green heads. Spawning females turn an olive green. Kokanee sometimes resemble the rainbow trout of large lakes in which both are often found. Kokanee, however, do not have spots, and their scales, which rub off easily, are smaller. Kokanee spawn in tributary streams

121

Continued on page 128

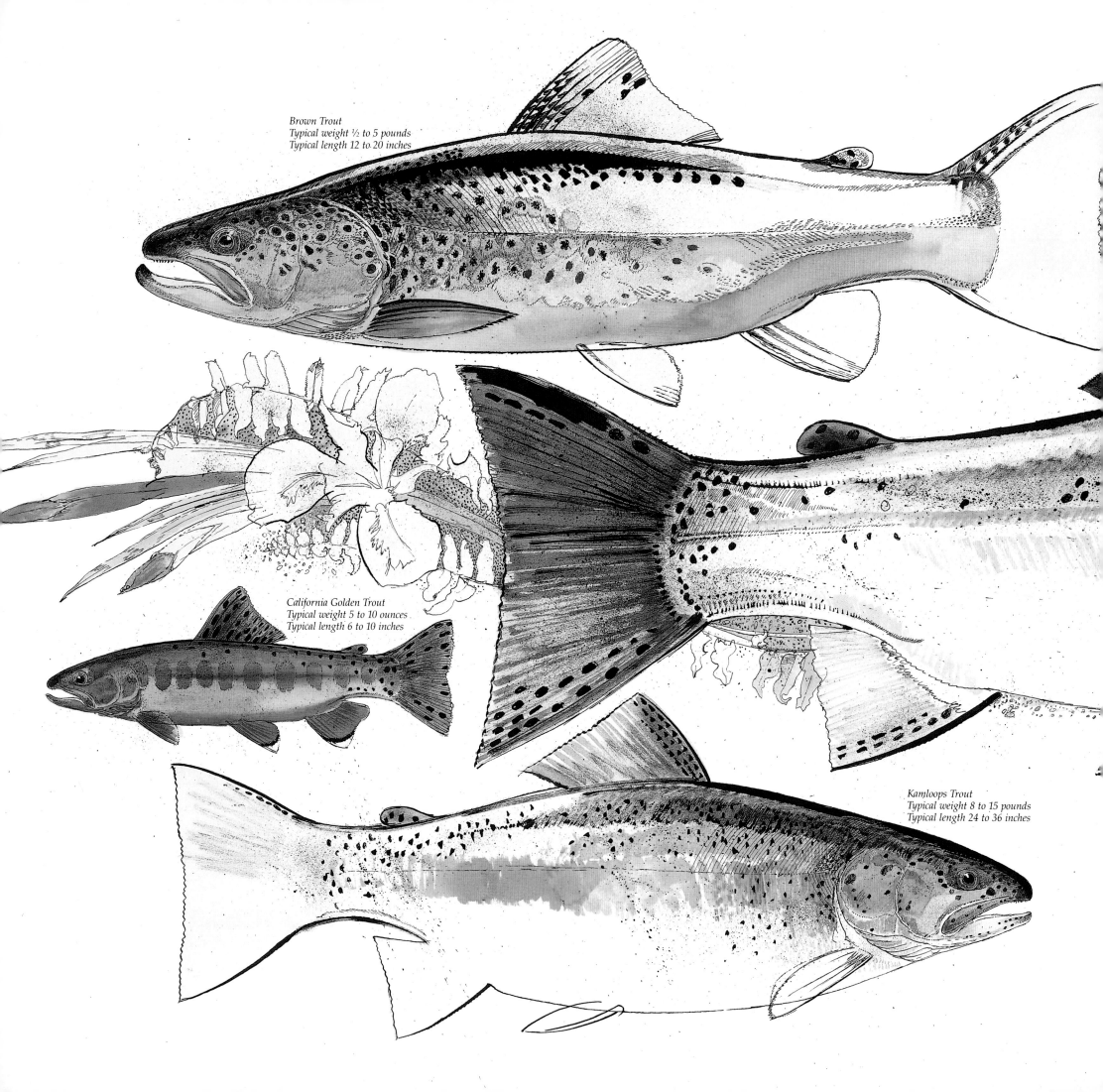

Brown Trout
Typical weight ½ to 5 pounds
Typical length 12 to 20 inches

California Golden Trout
Typical weight 5 to 10 ounces
Typical length 6 to 10 inches

Kamloops Trout
Typical weight 8 to 15 pounds
Typical length 24 to 36 inches

Yellowstone Cutthroat
Typical weight ½ to 4 pounds
Typical length 10 to 17 inches

Snake River Cutthroat
Typical weight ½ to 1 pound
Typical length 10 to 14 inches

Steelhead Trout
Typical weight 5 to 15 pounds
Typical length 20 to 36 inches

Rainbow Trout
Typical weight ½ to 5 pounds
Typical length 12 to 20 inches

Coastal Cutthroat
Typical weight 1 to 5 pounds
Typical length 14 to 20 inches

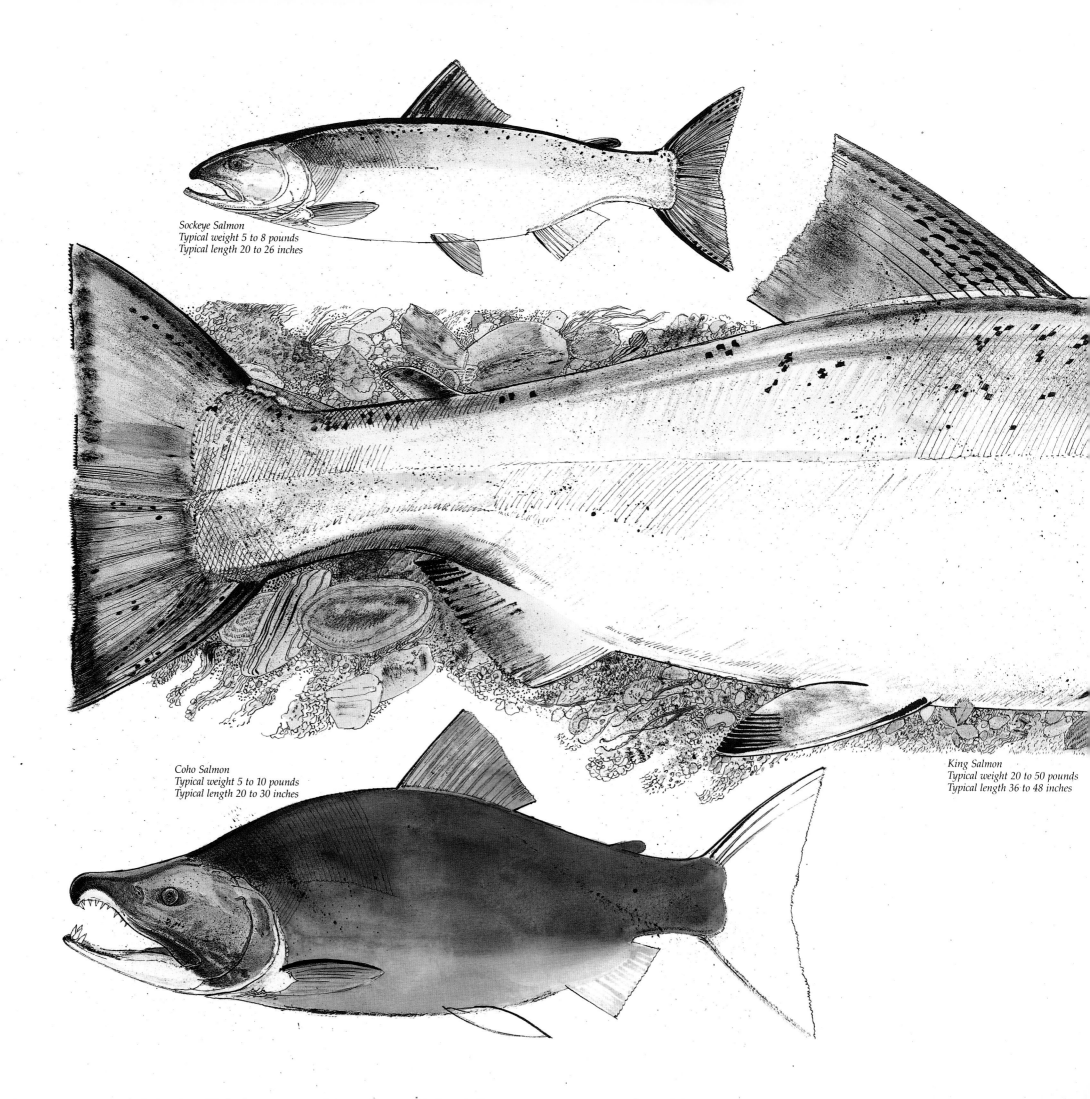

Sockeye Salmon
Typical weight 5 to 8 pounds
Typical length 20 to 26 inches

Coho Salmon
Typical weight 5 to 10 pounds
Typical length 20 to 30 inches

King Salmon
Typical weight 20 to 50 pounds
Typical length 36 to 48 inches

Chum Salmon
Typical weight 10 to 15 pounds
Typical length 24 to 30 inches

Humpback Salmon
Typical weight 3 to 5 pounds
Typical length 16 to 20 inches

Atlantic Salmon
Typical weight 8 to 40 pounds
Typical length 24 to 40 inches

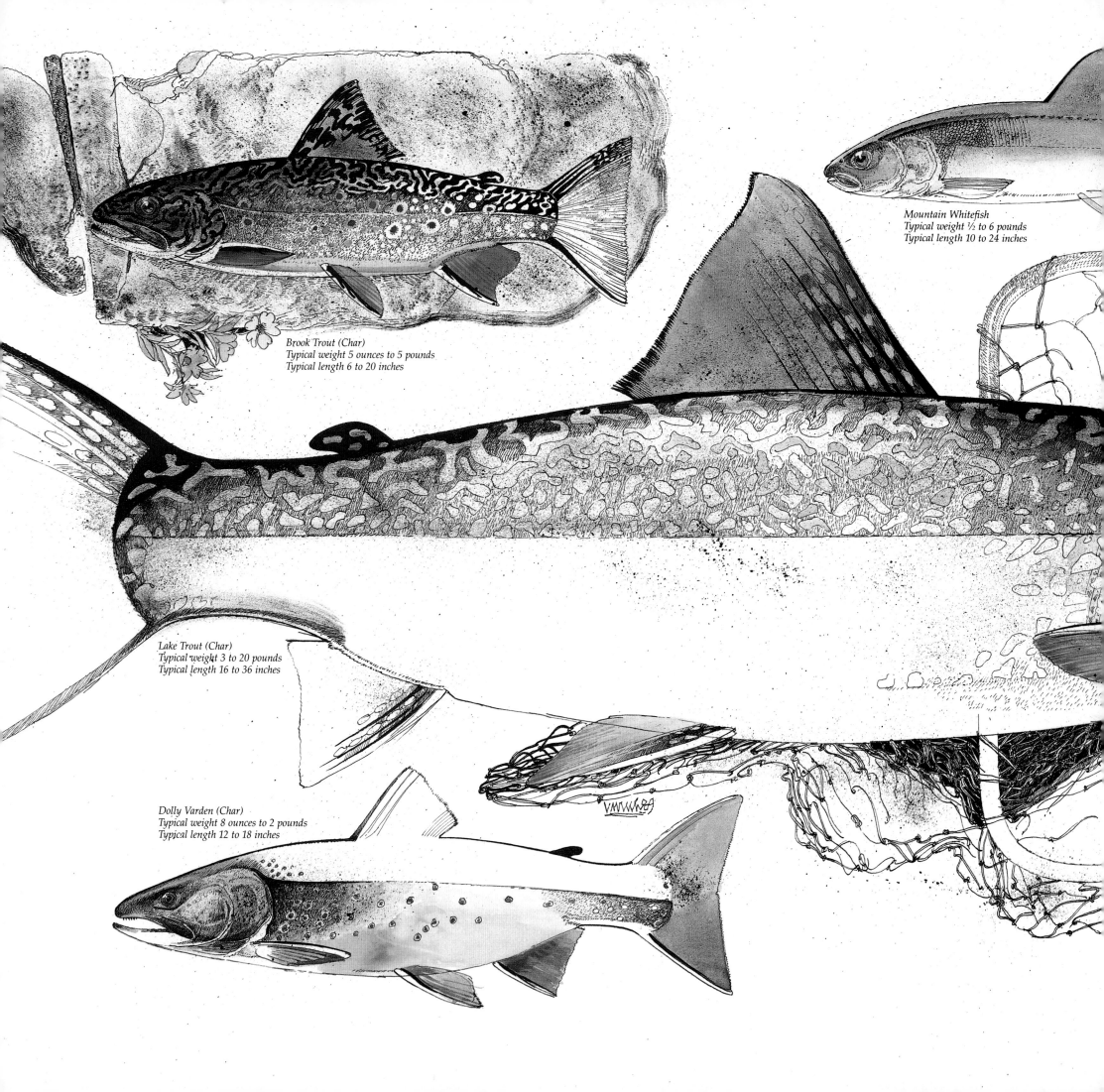

Brook Trout (Char)
Typical weight 5 ounces to 5 pounds
Typical length 6 to 20 inches

Mountain Whitefish
Typical weight ½ to 6 pounds
Typical length 10 to 24 inches

Lake Trout (Char)
Typical weight 3 to 20 pounds
Typical length 16 to 36 inches

Dolly Varden (Char)
Typical weight 8 ounces to 2 pounds
Typical length 12 to 18 inches

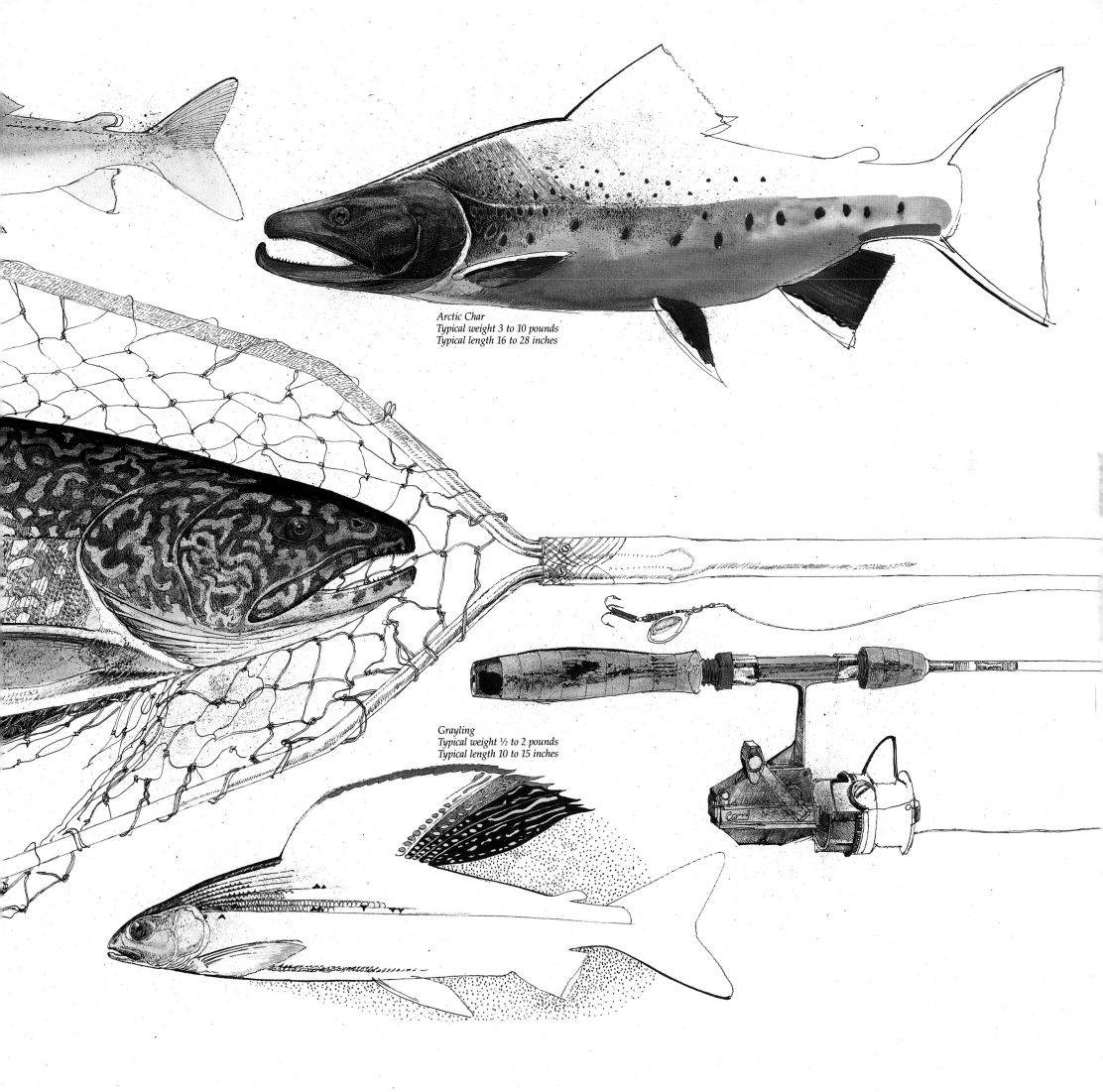

Arctic Char
Typical weight 3 to 10 pounds
Typical length 16 to 28 inches

Grayling
Typical weight ½ to 2 pounds
Typical length 10 to 15 inches

of the lakes where they are found, developing the same distinctive appearance as spawning sea-run salmon. Sockeye typically weigh five to eight pounds, with large ones in the fifteen-pound class, while kokanee typically range from ten to fourteen inches.

Coho (*Oncorhynchus kisutch*) are also commonly known as silver salmon. American runs range from Point Hope, Alaska to Monterey Bay, California. In addition, this Pacific rim native has been successfully transplanted into the Great Lakes, spawning in tributary rivers. In recent years attempts have been made to transplant Coho into eastern rivers with access to the Atlantic.

Coho have white gums and sparse spotting on the upper half of their tails. Spawning males darken rapidly, developing greenish heads and brown or maroon sides with a red lateral stripe. Females do not darken as much as males and do not develop the stripe. Coho weigh between five and ten pounds, with twenty pounds considered a large fish.

Humpback (*Oncorhynchus gorbusca*) are also known as humpy and pink salmon. They range from Alaska to Oregon, but their number diminishes greatly south of Puget Sound. Humpbacks get their name from the pronounced hump that develops in the back of the spawning male. They have tiny scales and a tail heavily marked with oval spots. Fresh pinks are silver-sided and have olive, black-spotted backs. The smallest of Pacific salmon, they typically weigh from three to five pounds, with a ten-pound pink being a rarity.

Atlantic salmon (*Salmo salar*), in its lake-resident form, is also known as landlock and ouananiche. Native of Europe and eastern

128

Appetites honed in the great outdoors must often be fed by stuff of questionable origin. Photograph by Tom Montgomery.

North America, ''the Leaper'' was once found in rivers far south on the east coast of the United States. Environmental degradation has drastically reduced its range. Atlantic Salmon are now found in limited numbers in New England, with the best North American runs appearing in the Maritime Provinces and the Gaspé region of Canada.

Atlantic salmon are silver-sided with dark blue or brown backs, and are distinguished by x-shaped spots. With spawning they darken, becoming nearly black. Unlike Pacific salmon, all of which die after spawning, some live to spawn again. The world-record Atlantic salmon weighed nearly eighty pounds, but typical fish caught in America weigh between eight and twenty pounds. Landlocks are considerably smaller, about two to four pounds.

CHAR

Brook trout (*Salvelinus fontinalis*) are also called brookie, brook char, squaretail, and speckled trout. In sea-running form it is the salter, and in the Great Lakes region, the coaster. The brookie is native to eastern North America, and is, in fact, not a true trout, but a char.

Brookies can be distinguished from trout by the presence of vermiculations (wormlike markings) on their backs. Brook trout are vividly colored with greenish backs that lighten on the sides, many bright yellow spots, and fewer red spots, which are rimmed in blue. Belly color may range from cream to vivid orange. Ventral fins are edged in white.

These fish have been transplanted widely throughout the United States. Although generally small, brookies are scrappy fighters. Stream-dwelling brookies are usually less than a foot in length, but in certain environments they grow to five pounds and more.

Lake trout (*Salvelinus namaycush*), also called laker and mackinaw, are native to Alaska and Canada, with native populations also appearing in north central and northeastern states. Lakers have been widely transplanted into large, deep, cold water lakes throughout the United States. Lake trout, actually char, are easily differentiated from trout by their light spots on a darker background. Their color ranges from olive green to gray, and they have deeply forked tails.

Lakers are usually large and deep-bodied. They can weigh over a hundred pounds (the current sport-fishing record stands at over sixty pounds); however, typical lake trout weigh from three to twenty pounds.

Arctic char (*Salvelinus alpinus*) exist in many varieties and, as a result, have many names. At one time several of these fish were considered separate species, but they have now been subsumed under the name arctic char. The various fish in this species include the landlocked New England blueback trout, the Sunapee golden trout, and the Quebec red trout, along with various other chars from northern regions. Arctic char are native to the northern parts of North America, Europe, and Asia. There are stream-resident, sea-running, and lake-dwelling forms.

The arctic char can be confused with the Dolly Varden, but is distinguished from this similar species by its forked tail, large spots, and long, sleek body. Alaskan arctic char typically weigh three to ten pounds. Eastern fish are considerably smaller.

Dolly Varden (*Salvelinus malma*). The nomenclature of the various Dolly Vardens is not resolved, but most biologists now agree that the anadromous Dolly Varden and the landlocked Dolly Varden are two different fish. The landlocked species is *Salvelinus confluentus* and is more typically called the bull trout. The sea-run variety is a native of the Pacific rim, with current populations existing from Washington north to Alaska. Fresh Dolly Varden exhibit silver sides and greenish backs, and they sport numerous red-orange spots, some with blue halos. Typical coastal Dolly Varden range from twelve to eighteen inches in length. The bull

Steelhead release by Jim Vincent.

trout is larger than the coastal variety, typically ranging from one to four pounds and its head is broader than that of the sea-run Dolly Varden. Bull trout are found in the northernmost western states, with the best populations occurring in the lakes of Montana, Idaho, Alaska, and British Columbia.

RELATED SPECIES

Grayling (*Thymallus arcticus*). American grayling, Montana grayling, Baikal grayling, and Kamchatka grayling, once considered separate species, are now all considered to be the same fish: *Thymallus arcticus*. These fish, whose native range included northern Siberia and northern North America (including Montana and Michigan), are rarely found in the United States

today in large self-sustaining populations. The one exception is Alaska. In Montana, Wyoming, and Utah relatively small, self-sustaining populations currently exist. They live in high altitude lakes and streams.

Their appearance is unique and virtually impossible to confuse with other fish. Dorsal fins of grayling are large and flowing, and present a kaleidoscope of color. Their scales are larger than those of trout, their tails deeply forked, and their mouths small. Because of the limited food available in their habitat and the short period of full feeding activity (winters are long in the arctic environment), grayling grow slowly. A three-year-old fish might reach twelve inches in length; a five-year-old, fifteen inches.

Mountain whitefish (*Prosopium williamsoni*) are also called whitefish and Rocky Mountain whitefish. Mountain whitefish belong to a family of whitefish known to most anglers because of its tendency to inhabit the same waters as trout.

They have large scales, small mouths, deeply forked tails, and their backs are usually a brown that blends to silver on the sides. Their bodies are free of spots.

Typical whitefish are ten or eleven inches in length, but some become much larger in favorable habitat. 🐟

NOTE: Effective January 1, 1989, the American Fisheries Society announced the following changes in nomenclature:
  • Pacific trout and salmon now belong to the genus *oncorhynchus*.
  • Rainbow and steelhead species have changed from *gairdneri* to *mykyss*.
These changes reflect research in tissue analysis and phyllogenetic history. However, the author and publisher have elected to stay with the former nomenclature to avoid confusion until the changes have had time to become generally known.

129

TACKLE

You can catch trout with a stick, some string, and a hook if you know what you're doing, but you'd miss a big part of the pleasure of fly-fishing: the wonderful feeling that comes from casting a fine rod or playing fish on a beautifully made reel.

Tackle, to an angler, ranks pretty high in the scheme of things, and I don't think this has anything to do with materialism or snobbery. Many of us use and cherish a graceful bamboo or graphite fly rod, an elegant British fly reel, and not all of us, by any means, are wealthy. The love of fine tackle has little to do with finances. Like so much in the world of trouting, it has more to do with aesthetics.

Tackle has a long history. Fly-fishing began with a technique we now know as dapping. A fixed length of line was attached to a long rod fashioned from solid wood, and the fly was dropped on the water. The line was a knotted bundle of animal hair, and a reel was not necessary. Later, lengthening and shortening the line was done with a winch, or reel, and guides were added to rods so that this could be accomplished. Early reels were nothing more than arbors with handles, set inside cages. Rod guides, at the time, consisted of simple rings. This rod and reel combination served us well for centuries, until we decided that we wanted to cast the fly, and at this point the evolution of fly-fishing equipment began to change rapidly.

The first casting rods were fashioned from solid wood, usually greenheart hickory. They were whippy and slow. False casting and line shooting were difficult. Dry fly-fishing required accurate placement of the fly and a sufficient line speed to allow the false casting that would dry the fly—something had to be done.

The split-cane fly rod began its evolution in England in the mid-nineteenth century, but a truly powerful cane rod did not emerge until late in the century, and it came from the shop of an American, a Pennsylvanian named Samuel Phillipe. Phillipe, a violin maker and gunsmith, was also an angler. He applied his keen mind and great fabricating skills to the problem of building a better fly rod, and came up with something entirely new: a split-cane rod built from sections of bamboo, glued together with the power fibers located on the outside of the rod. The British deserve to be credited with the invention of the split-bamboo rod, but it was Phillipe who first placed the hard exterior of the cane on the outside of the rod, placing the pithy center of the bamboo in the rod's center. The result was a rod with great power, low weight, and what Vincent Marinaro has called "a cushioned stroke." The pithy center added little strength, but did dampen vibration and soften even a powerful cast. Many anglers prefer a bamboo rod just for this property.

Natural materials were dominant in the manufacture of rods until early in the twentieth century, when, in an attempt to make more affordable rods available, tubular steel rods were made. Steel rods were relatively heavy and didn't cast as well as bamboo, but they were practically indestructible. Nearly anyone could afford to buy one.

World War II gave us many technological advances, including a strange fabrication process using hairlike fibers of glass held together in a matrix of plastic resin—fiberglass. In the quest for the perfect fly rod, fiberglass was an obvious material to try. Fiberglass, like tubular steel, was strong and elastic; moreover, it was lighter than steel and not susceptible to rust. The early fiberglass rods were made from solid sticks of fiberglass, and they cast like clubs. It was soon discovered, however, that a light, quick-casting rod resulted from forming fiberglass over a mandrel, a pattern that held the shape of the rod's taper. A variety of mass-

Atlantic Salmon, Gaula River, Norway by R. Valentine Atkinson/Frontiers.

130

produced, hollow fiberglass rods that cast quite well, emerged on the angling scene.

This same process, the forming of a synthetic rod over a solid mandrel, is still in use, but a tremendous proliferation of materials is amenable to the process.

Carbon (also known as graphite) fibers have come to us courtesy of the aerospace industry, where strength and lightness are mandatory. Graphite rods are believed by many to be the best casting implements ever made. Of all the materials used for fly rods, carbon fiber has the greatest strength with the least weight. It can be tapered to allow a variety of actions. Its resistance to bending and speed of recovery after being bent are extraordinary, and this translates into the ability to create high line speeds and long casts. Carbon fiber can make a well-dampened rod, eliminating unwanted vibrations quickly, and it is durable.

Fly-fishing rods are selected according to several parameters. Material choice has a great deal to do with individual preference and budget. A rod that will perform satisfactorily can be fashioned from any of the three dominant materials. But the choice of line weight and rod length is even more critical.

Until recently, anglers matched lines to rods by feel. This is largely no longer the case. Modern rods carry a line-size designation that specifies the line weight the manufacturer has designed the rod to cast. The designation is a number from one to twelve. Low numbers are used for light lines, and high numbers for heavy lines. Most anglers fish four to seven weights for trout, and seven to ten weights for salmon and steelhead.

The second important variable in rod se-

Salmon gear by R. Valentine Atkinson/Frontiers.

lection is length. Arguments about rod length abound. In the good old days (at the turn of the century), a rod of less than nine feet in length was pretty unusual. In fact, a nine-footer was considered a short rod. As time passed rods became shorter, until about twenty-five years ago, when extremely short rods enjoyed a sudden popularity. One champion of the short rod, Lee Wulff, took the short rod to an extreme—casting a line, hooking, landing, and releasing an Atlantic salmon with no rod at all! He used his bare hands!

The question of rod length involves sev-

eral issues. The primary factor in favor of short rods is weight. A six-foot rod can be made much lighter than a ten-footer. The argument has been made that a light rod is more fun to fish because it is less tiring to cast. Short rods are believed by many to be better in heavy brush. Finally, it is easier to make a short rod with an extremely fast action, and some anglers prefer this type of rod.

Long rod devotees have a few arguments of their own. Long rods may be a bit heavier, but a longer rod allows more effortless casting. One of the most important aspects of fishing, as opposed to casting, is controlling the fly and line after they have landed on the water. A long rod excels at holding line out of water that is faster or slower than the water where you wish to fish your fly. Longer rods allow corrective action, such as line mending, to be made with less effort. Keeping a cast above streamside brush with a long rod is often easier than with a short one, so the merits of a short rod in dense brush may be overstated. Most trout rods used today fall between eight and nine feet in length.

Steelhead and salmon rods have a few special requirements. Their ability to play fish is often as important as their ability to cast long distances. Although trout rods are designed for single-handed use, salmon rods can be either single- or double-handed. The two-handed salmon rod is the standard salmon fishing implement in Europe. These rods, often fourteen feet long, place the reel well up on the rod and surround it on each side with cork grips. One hand is placed above the reel, and the other below. Casting is accomplished with both hands, and with such a rod and two-

Continued on page 134

131

One of the most sensual experiences in fly-fishing comes from casting a fine fly rod, or playing a fish on a beautifully crafted reel. Quality in any object is expensive. But the use of such aesthetically pleasing equipment transcends material value. Photograph by John Oldenkamp and Cynthia Sabransky.

Canoe fishing, Little Redfish Lake, Idaho by David Stoecklein.

134

handed casting techniques, casts of great distance are possible with significantly less false casting than with the single-handed rod. With line manipulation, control of a salmon fly drift is greatly enhanced. When a fish is hooked, it is an easy matter to use the portion of the rod below the reel as a brace, playing the fish from the reel, which is perfectly situated, well away from the body. On single-handed rods, a fighting butt is often installed below the reel seat to ease bracing the rod against the body.

While rods have changed dramatically in the past fifty years, the standard trout reel remains remarkably like the one our ancestors used. There are three basic types of trout reels. Single-action reels retrieve one coil of line with each rotation of the reel handle. Single-action reels are simple, light, and reliable. For most fishermen they are the reel of choice. With a counterbalanced spool, a good drag system, and when sized to take an appropriate line and quantity of backing, they can be used for any fish stalked with the fly.

A variation on the single-action reel is the multiplying reel. These reels, slightly heavier, but similar in appearance and design to single-action reels, contain a gearing mechanism that causes the spool to rotate several times with each rotation of the handle. Multipliers are not nearly as common as single-action reels, but they are used by many anglers.

Finally, there are automatic reels. These reels contain a spring mechanism that coils line upon the pressing of a lever. Automatic reels have little controllable drag, and they are prone to malfunction at the worst possible moment. I do not recommend their use for trout or salmon.

The last major item of fly tackle is the fly line. Like the rod, it has changed a great deal with the passage of time. The earliest lines consisted of knotted animal hair. A significant improvement occurred after the braided-silk lines appeared. Silk lines were used for a long time, and are used today by a few who enjoy their feel, but there are some serious drawbacks associated with silk. Treated silk lines will float, but even the best treatments don't keep water out for very long. Sometime during the course of an average fishing day a silk line has to be stripped from the reel, and dried in the sun. Silk lines are very difficult to find, and the range of sizes and tapers is limited. They are also extraordinarily expensive.

Modern plastic lines remedy these problems admirably, and although they lack silk's ability to be selectively waterproofed (floating or sinking as chosen by the angler), most modern fishermen do not miss this feature. Floating lines that always float and sinking lines that predictably sink are vast improvements on the quirks and difficulties of silk.

Fly lines are probably the least glamorous major item of fly tackle, but they are by no means the least important. In many ways, the choice of a fly line is the most significant choice an angler will make. Choice revolves around a few basic properties: whether or not the line floats, its weight, its taper, and its color.

The basic line for all anglers is the floating line, used to present flies on the surface, just below the surface, or fairly deep with appropriate weight applied to the leader. Not all fishing situations can be handled with a floating line, however, and two broad categories of sinking lines exist to fill the gap. Lines that sink along their entire length are called full-sinking lines, or simply, sinking lines, and they are made in several densities that allow fishing at many different depths. Lines that sink at the tip, but float otherwise, are called sink-tip lines, and they too are made in various densities. Sink-tip lines are available with various lengths of sinking-tip. A sink-tip line is much easier to control on the water than a full-sinking line. The floating portion can be mended, it can be watched for indications of a strike, and it can be more easily lifted from the water for another cast.

Line weight is determined by the weight of the first thirty feet of line. This weight, expressed in a system of numbers on a scale of one to twelve, matches the scale used for rods. The number says nothing about how weight is distributed along a line: this variable is known as taper.

At one time most fishermen used a level line, one that is of consistent diameter. This type of line is easy to manufacture, and therefore is inexpensive, but it has some serious drawbacks. The most significant is that a level line simply does not cast well; another is its inability to present a fly with delicacy.

Most fishermen now use tapered lines. Line tapers are calculated to provide a balance between the weight distribution needed for casting, the line weight needed for line control methods such as mending, and the delicacy at the point required for gentle fly presentation. Modern tapers accomplish these goals admirably. The basic tapers are the double-taper, which emphasizes line control and delicacy of presentation, and the weight-forward, which emphasizes the ability to cast longer distances.

The last variable, line color, is to my mind the least important. Although I doubt it matters a great deal to trout, color has some significance to the angler. Most of us fish better when we are able to see what our line is doing; consequently, most floating fly lines are now made in bright colors.

A good fisherman chooses tackle carefully and with substantial knowledge of its properties. Nothing is less fun than trying to fish with poorly matched equipment or equipment ill-suited to the task at hand. Having a properly selected rig, however, makes the intrusion of tackle minimal. With good equipment, fishing becomes what it should be: a matter between you and the fish. 🪝

Lewis Lake, Yellowstone National Park, Wyoming by Terry Ring.

FLIES

This business of tying feathers and fur to a hook, and using the artificial fly to catch trout, is a lot older than many people realize. Written record of the subject extends back at least to the time of Alexander the Great, but the artificial fly likely existed even before this rather ancient date. The first major literary work in English regarding the artificial fly was written by a nun from Sopwell, England at the end of the fifteenth century, and from that time to the present the history of the artificial fly has been well documented.

An old saying about French politics goes, "Wherever three Frenchmen are present, you have four political parties." The same is true of fly-fishermen. Give me an insect on the water and three fly-casters, and I guarantee at least four different artificials would be produced to imitate it. Give me three fly-fishermen, and I bet they'd also produce four theories about why their flies work. Fly-fishing has had as many controversies as there have been anglers. Most of the controversies center on the artificial fly and its presentation to the trout.

Imitation. Presentation. These two words sum up centuries of fly-fishing thought. We observe that trout attempt to eat our artificial flies, but there is, by no means, any universal agreement about why. A strict imitationist would argue that a trout attempts to eat an artificial fly because the fish believes it not only to be edible, but to be, in fact, a specific insect it has eaten before. A strict presentationist argues that we cannot be certain what a trout thinks it is eating when it takes an artificial fly, but we know it will take certain artificials when they are made to behave properly. Few anglers take a hard line on either of these positions, but the design of flies, and the choice of materials and colors are significantly influenced by where we lean on this question of imitation versus presentation. Those who favor imitation strive to mimic the appearance of specific insects. Those who lean toward presentation usually fish a few carefully chosen and broadly suggestive designs.

When anglers have been asked to rate the significant properties of a fly they mention many things, but most lists usually boil down to the same attributes, ranked in the same order of importance. The behavior of the fly is

Fall reflections, Swift River, New Hampshire by Willard Clay.

paramount (to fish a floating fly is useless, for example, when fish are actively feeding on the bottom of a stream). Next are size and shape (a fish taking large nymphs would most likely be caught on a large fly shaped like a nymph). Then comes color.

Many years ago and well into this century, most flies actually fished in this country were what we now call attractor flies. They were flies that caught fish, but we would have been hard-pressed to say what creatures the flies imitated. Many artificials were tied in gaudy colors, with shiny gold and silver tinsels. Attractors, for the most part, have fallen out of favor, largely because they are no longer effective. Fish have known greater angling pressure, and have seen more artificial flies, so catching them with attractors has become more difficult. Most serious fly-fishermen now fish with specific imitations of particular species or with less specifically imitative flies (but flies that are imitative, nonetheless), either of which are significantly more effective than the older, more colorful, attractor flies.

Wild fish in remote places seldom if ever see anglers or artificial flies, and for those fish, life depends on finding food. They'll take just about any fly that comes their way. They are often wild and wary, but they haven't been stuck by artificials. Other fish, more exposed to angling, that live in waters where a wide variety of foods are continuously present, will accept a reasonably wide range of patterns and sizes, but flies that imitate an available food source will be more successful than those that do not. The most difficult fish, and for many the most fun to pursue, are those that have experienced a great deal of angling pressure

Rods and flies by R. Valentine Atkinson/Frontiers.

and feed selectively on specific insects during periods when those insects are available in large numbers. These fish can be maddeningly discriminating about artificial flies, and the choice of a fly pattern and design can be critical. The manner in which a fly is presented is almost always significant, and the design and pattern of a fly become more and more important as we angle for increasingly selective fish.

Design refers to a fly's general appearance and behavior on, or in, the water. Design decisions include choice of materials, how and where they will be applied, and the shape and look of the fly. The difference between a wet fly and a dry fly, for example, is one of design. Wet flies are tied with materials that readily absorb water, or in some way enhance the ability of a fly to sink. Dry flies use nonabsorbent materials or have some other property that makes them float. Wet flies have heavy hooks, dry flies light ones. Wet flies use softer hackles, dry flies stiff ones. To a great extent, traditional wet flies share the same design as traditional dry flies; differences relate largely to matters of color, and are actually differences of pattern. Modern flies often differ widely from the traditional wet fly and dry fly. Innovative fly designs include new uses for old materials, new placement of these materials and the altering of traditional proportions, as well as the introduction of radically new materials like foam rubber, and polypropylene.

The principal reality affecting fly design today is the same as it was centuries ago—we are simply using new methods and materials to respond to it. Factors that influence our designs relate directly to our understanding of the forage present in the cold water habitat and the way trout feed. Our knowledge of the complexity of aquatic life has increased tremendously, and the changes in our flies represent a response to this growth.

Widely used flies exist within the context of a good many standard designs (and a mindboggling variety of patterns within these design categories). In addition, any trout fishing region worthy of the label has a multitude of locally tied imitations that are rarely seen elsewhere. Any attempt at a thorough catalog of these flies would be extraordinarily difficult. The flies reproduced here sketch a broad outline within which various designs and patterns exist, and flesh out that outline with some of the more popular examples. The flies shown represent some of the most familiar to anglers, flies most often used, and some design variations that have emerged in the past few years.

There is no reason why an angler should fish only those flies designed by others. One of the great joys of angling is the attempt to design your own flies for your own waters, flies that work for you on your own fish—flies that have evolved from your own experience and have come from the jaws of your own vise.

137

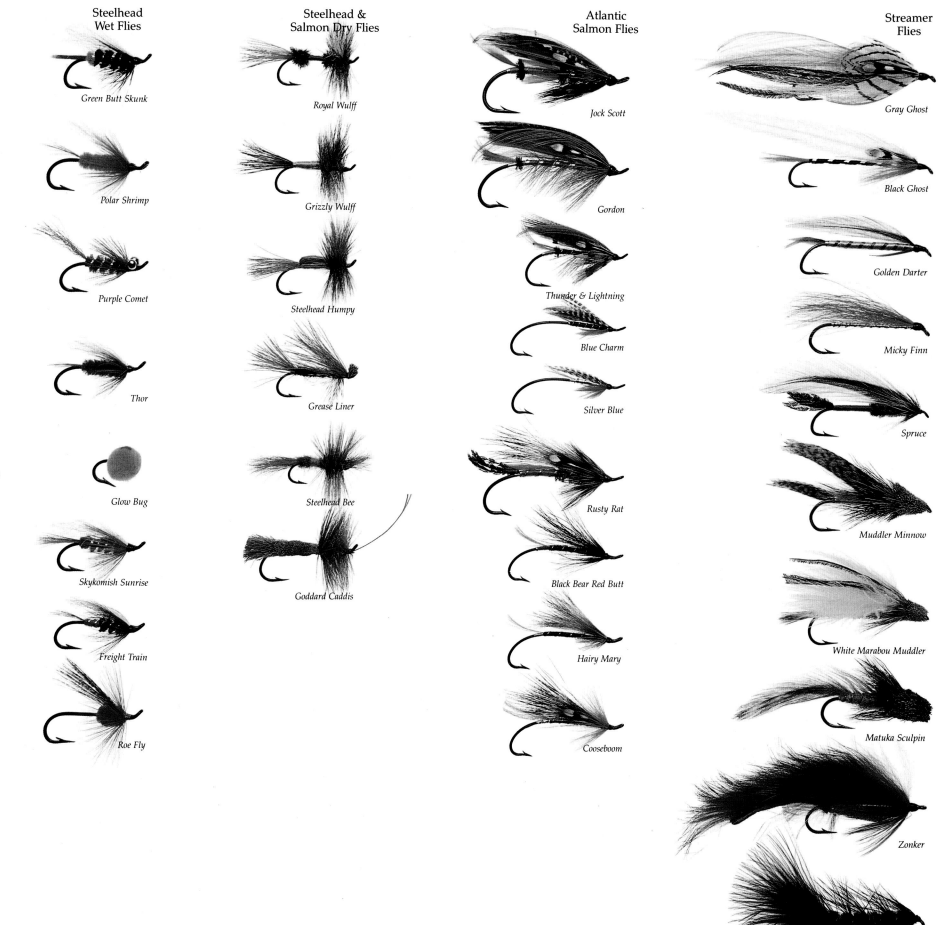

Steelhead Wet Flies

Green Butt Skunk

Polar Shrimp

Purple Comet

Thor

Glow Bug

Skykomish Sunrise

Freight Train

Roe Fly

138

Steelhead & Salmon Dry Flies

Royal Wulff

Grizzly Wulff

Steelhead Humpy

Grease Liner

Steelhead Bee

Goddard Caddis

Atlantic Salmon Flies

Jock Scott

Gordon

Thunder & Lightning

Blue Charm

Silver Blue

Rusty Rat

Black Bear Red Butt

Hairy Mary

Cooseboom

Streamer Flies

Gray Ghost

Black Ghost

Golden Darter

Micky Finn

Spruce

Muddler Minnow

White Marabou Muddler

Matuka Sculpin

Zonker

Wooly Bugger

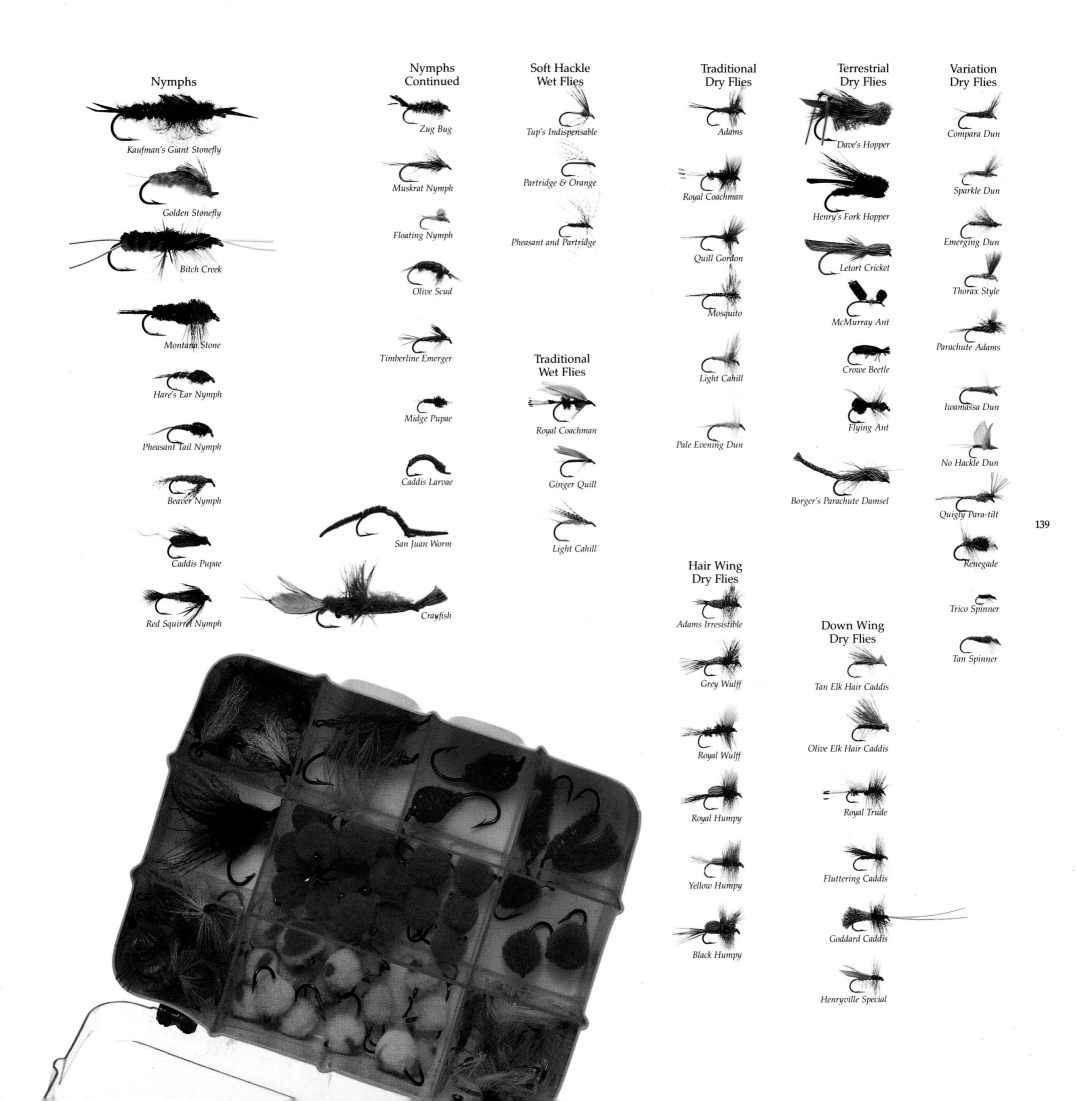

Nymphs

Kaufman's Giant Stonefly

Golden Stonefly

Bitch Creek

Montana Stone

Hare's Ear Nymph

Pheasant Tail Nymph

Beaver Nymph

Caddis Pupae

Red Squirrel Nymph

Nymphs Continued

Zug Bug

Muskrat Nymph

Floating Nymph

Olive Scud

Timberline Emerger

Midge Pupae

Caddis Larvae

San Juan Worm

Crayfish

Soft Hackle Wet Flies

Tup's Indispensable

Partridge & Orange

Pheasant and Partridge

Traditional Wet Flies

Royal Coachman

Ginger Quill

Light Cahill

Traditional Dry Flies

Adams

Royal Coachman

Quill Gordon

Mosquito

Light Cahill

Pale Evening Dun

Hair Wing Dry Flies

Adams Irresistible

Grey Wulff

Royal Wulff

Royal Humpy

Yellow Humpy

Black Humpy

Terrestrial Dry Flies

Dave's Hopper

Henry's Fork Hopper

Letort Cricket

McMurray Ant

Crowe Beetle

Flying Ant

Borger's Parachute Damsel

Down Wing Dry Flies

Tan Elk Hair Caddis

Olive Elk Hair Caddis

Royal Trude

Fluttering Caddis

Goddard Caddis

Henryville Special

Variation Dry Flies

Compara Dun

Sparkle Dun

Emerging Dun

Thorax Style

Parachute Adams

Iwamassa Dun

No Hackle Dun

Quigly Para-tilt

Renegade

Trico Spinner

Tan Spinner

140

Henry's Fork of the Snake River, Idaho by Kitty Pearson-Vincent.

Bibliography

Bergman, Ray. *Trout*. Alfred A. Knopf, Inc., New York, 1938.

Brooks, Charles E. *Larger Trout for the Western Fly Fisherman*. Nick Lyons Books/Winchester Press, Piscataway, N.J., 1983.

Combs, Trey. *Steelhead Fly Fishing and Flies*. Frank Amato Publications, Portland, Ore., 1976.

Dunham, Judith. *The Art of the Trout Fly*. Chronicle Books, San Francisco, 1988.

Gierach, John. *Trout Bum*. Pruett Publishing Co., Boulder, 1986.

Gingrich, Arnold, ed. *American Trout Fishing by Theodore Gordon and a Company of Anglers*. Alfred A. Knopf, Inc., New York, 1966.

Gordon, Sid W. *How to Fish from Top to Bottom*. Stackpole Books, Harrisburg, Pa., 1955.

Haig-Brown, Roderick L. *A River Never Sleeps*. Nick Lyons Books/Winchester Press, Piscátaway, N.J., 1974.

———. *Fisherman's Fall*. Douglas & McIntyre, Ltd., Vancouver, B.C., 1975.

———. *Return to the River: The Story of the Chinook Run*. Willow Creek Press, Oshkosh, Wis., 1984.

Hewitt, Edward R. *A Trout & Salmon Fisherman for Seventy-five Years*. Van Cortland Press, Croton-on-Hudson, N.Y., 1972.

Humphrey, William. *My Moby Dick*. Doubleday & Co., Inc., New York, 1978.

Krieger, Mel. *The Essence of Flycasting*. Club Pacific, San Francisco, 1987.

LaFontaine, Gary. *Challenge of the Trout*. Mountain Press Publishing Co., Missoula, Mont., 1976.

Lampman, Ben Hur. *A Leaf from French Eddy: A Collection of Essays on Fish, Anglers & Fishermen*. Harper & Row, Publishers, San Francisco, 1979.

Lee, Art. *Fishing Dry Flies for Trout on Rivers and Streams*. Atheneum, New York, 1983.

Leisenring, James E., and Vernon S. Hidy. *The Art of Tying the Wet Fly and Fishing the Flymph*. Crown Publishers, Inc., New York, 1971.

Leiser, Eric. *The Complete Book of Fly Tying*. Alfred A. Knopf, Inc., New York, 1981.

Leonard, J. Edson. *Feather in the Breeze*. Freshet Press, Rockville Center, N.Y., 1974.

Lyons, Nick. *The Seasonable Angler: Journeys Through a Fisherman's Year*. Winchester Press, Piscataway, N.J., 1970.

McCafferty, W. Patrick. *Aquatic Entomology: The Fisherman's and Ecologist's Illustrated Guide to Insects and Their Relatives*. Science Books International, Boston, 1981.

Maclean, Norman. *A River Runs Through It and Other Stories*. University of Chicago Press, Chicago, 1976.

Marinaro, Vincent C. *In the Ring of the Rise*. Crown Publishers, Inc., New York, 1976.

———. *A Modern Dry Fly Code*. Crown Publishers, Inc., New York, 1950.

McMillan, Bill. *Dry Line Steelhead and Other Subjects*. Frank Amato Publications, Portland, Ore., 1987.

Nemes, Sylvester. *The Soft-Hackled Fly*. The Chatham Press, Old Greenwich, Conn., 1975.

Proper, Datus C. *What the Trout Said: About the Design of Trout Flies and Other Mysteries*. Alfred A. Knopf, Inc., New York, 1982.

Raymond, Steve. *The Year of the Anglers*. Winchester Press, Piscataway, N.J., 1983.

Schwiebert, Ernest. *Death of a Riverkeeper*. Donald S. Ellis/Creative Arts Book Company, San Francisco, 1984.

———. *Matching the Hatch*. Macmillan Publishing Co., Inc., New York, 1955.

———. *Remembrances of Rivers Past*. The Macmillan Company, New York, 1972.

———. *Trout*. E. P. Dutton, Inc., New York, 1978.

Stroud, Tully. *Trout Chaser's Journal: A Diary for the Trout & Salmon Fisherman*. Chronicle Books, San Francisco, 1986.

Traver, Robert. *Trout Madness*. St. Martin's Press, New York, 1960.

———. *Trout Magic*. Crown Publishers, Inc., New York, 1974.

Wetherell, W. D. *Vermont River*. Nick Lyons Books/Winchester Press, Piscataway, N.J., 1984.

Wright, Leonard M., Jr. *Fly Fishing Heresies: A New Gospel for American Anglers*. Stoeger Publishing Co., South Hackensack, N.J., 1975.

Wulff, Joan Salvato. *Joan Wulff's Fly Casting Techniques*. Nick Lyons Books, New York, 1987.

Wulff, Lee. *Trout on a Fly*. Nick Lyons Books, New York, 1986.

Zahner, Don. *Anglish Spoken Here*. The Stephen Greene Press, Lexington, Mass., 1986.

142

Streamside Reflections was produced in association with the publisher by McQuiston & Partners in Del Mar, California: art direction, Don McQuiston; editorial supervision, Tom Chapman; mechanical production, Joyce Sweet and Kristi Paulson; copyediting, Robin Witkin and Frankie Wright; composition, TypeLink; text type, Palatino designed by Hermann Zapf; text paper is 157-gsm Glossy Coated; printed in Japan by Dai Nippon Printing Co., Ltd.

Rainbow from Silver Creek, Idaho by David Stoecklein.